Bernard Haldane Associates'
JOB & CAREER BUILDING

Bernard Haldane Associates'
JOB & CAREER BUILDING

by Richard Germann
& Peter Arnold

Ten Speed Press

Ten Speed Press
P O Box 7123
Berkeley, California 94707

Cover Design by Brenton Beck

ISBN: 0-89815-048-5
Library of Congress Catalog Number: 81-51898

10   9   8   7   6   5   4   3   2   1

Contents

Introduction

Have you ever watched the faces of people going to work on a Monday morning? The first time I did, I had a traumatic experience. It was a hot Monday in July many years ago on the subway going to my job in downtown New York City. As I watched the people sitting and standing opposite me, I was overwhelmed with the expressions of misery, resignation, and quiet desperation on their faces. This memory has haunted me ever since.

I have spent the past fifteen years attempting to help as many people as possible escape the "Monday Morning Horrors." Most of my early work was done in one-to-one counseling sessions; later in training job and career counselors and in developing new approaches to job and career counseling. This book is the result of that work. It is written to enable you to take control of your job and your career.

A word about the clients I and my many associates have worked with—of all the people who quietly (or not so quietly) suffer from a multitude of job and career problems, it is our clients who have had the courage to take positive action. They are the ones who have said "No" to the idea that work is a necessary evil; "No" that luck and the employer control their lives; and "No" that they must settle for what they can get.

I welcome you to the growing body of men and women who are determined to take control of their lives.

It would not have been possible to write this book without the combined knowledge, as well as the specific assistance, of a large number of men and women. I am delighted to acknowledge the contributions of our firm's founder, Bernard Haldane, who originated and developed the concept and systems associated with studying achievements and successes to identify transferable skills and talents. This is the concept on which modern career counseling is based. I must also acknowledge Eli Djeddah, Earl Bark, and Saul Gruner, who joined Dr. Haldane fourteen years later and helped establish much of the groundwork for the present Haldane organization. I also want to acknowledge the contributions made by Lowell Martin, David Eysmann, Earl Bark, Dan Bruce, and Jay Pugh, as well as Bob Lavin, Larry Miller, and George Klein, who helped build the organization through which these job and career concepts could be tested, further developed, and applied to our clients' benefit.

The current state of the career-development profession, as reflected in this book, is based on the work of the entire counseling leadership and staff of the Haldane organization. I wish to specifically thank Carl Armbruster, Wes Merritt, Howard Payne, John Shreve, and Jim Taylor, as well as Arthur Pearson, John Heard, Harold Gallagher, Tony Perna, and Ray Canalini, who have worked and are working throughout the United States to advance job and career concepts and bring them to an increasing number of working men and women.

The final shape of this book was heavily influenced by the thoughtful contributions of Jeanne Onorato McGuire, who has helped us stay in close touch with developments in the work world, and of our Public Information Director, Diane Blumenson, who, together with our Communications Director, Stephen Fischer, has brought many of these job and career development concepts to the public through public service programs.

I thank Natalie Dawes, Ellen Cox, and Linda Gerber for their dedication to getting the manuscript into publishable form, and Max Gartenberg and Harold Grove for helping information on this vital subject to reach the public.

And, finally, I express my gratitude to my co-author, Peter Arnold, without whose initiative, good judgment, and hard work this book would not exist, and to my wife, Sheridan, for her intelligent interest, ideas, and encouragement.

RICHARD GERMANN
Boston

1
Myths and Facts

How much do you learn from your mistakes? Is it true that the squeaky wheel always gets the grease? Will a career change cost you money?

As you begin the adventure of job and career building, take a look at common assumptions about jobs and careers that you may have taken for facts as long as you can remember. Those assumptions turn out to be myths, on closer examination. They have very little to do with the realities of the world of work.

Over the last thirty years, Haldane clients have learned that when the job and career myths with which they grew up have been replaced by the facts presented in this book, their careers have taken a noticeable jump forward.

You are the beneficiary of the spadework done by more than 55,000 job seekers and career builders.

Here are some of the most common myths, as well as the facts to replace them in your thinking.

Myth: Careers just happen.
Fact: Careers are planned—or they won't happen. What happens instead is a series of accidents—some of them lucky—most of them not.

1

The saddest thing in the world is a man or woman at age fifty-plus who finds that the thread has snapped. We see many such individuals. They always found it easy to get reasonably decent jobs. Suddenly, it isn't easy. They never gave any thought to career planning, and now the only visible direction of their employment history leads to old age.

A continuous career, incidentally, is not necessarily related to continuous paid employment. Being a housewife, for instance, can be very much a part of a solid career.

Myth: You learn from your career mistakes.

Fact: All you learn from your mistakes is what *not* to do. They don't tell you what to do. The founder of professional career counseling in the United States, Bernard Haldane, has established that the study of individual successes, not failures, is the most valuable tool in career planning.

Myth: Career changes are risky and expensive.

Fact: Your new career, if correctly planned, uses more of your recognized talents and skills and is more in tune with your personality. You will do a better job and be worth more to your employer.

Forty-eight percent of Haldane clients who changed careers experienced an immediate increase in income on starting their second careers. But there are ground rules. It doesn't happen by accident.

Myth: The job market dictates what career you should choose. Go only into a growth field.

Fact: This myth has been responsible for more failure and misery than any other. A career is not built on what's good out there, but on what's good in *you*.

Myth: Tests can tell you what you should be doing for the rest of your life.

Fact: No one can tell you what you should do. In the hands of an experienced professional counselor, a good vocational or psychological test is one of many tools to help you recognize a career direction. Only you can make a career decision.

Myth: Women do better in careers that are traditionally held by women.

Fact: Women have as wide a range of talents, skills, and motivating factors as men. Limited career choice means limited access to a productive, fulfilling career.

The belief that women are best suited for the jobs commonly held by women is a matter of tradition, not reality. There are undoubtedly a few jobs in which women can be more productive, as there are certain tasks that men can accomplish better. But the tradition of assigning certain professions to one sex or the other has very little to do with reality. You may need to overcome a few obstacles in generating job offers in some areas, but those difficulties are diminishing every day. Don't allow them to interfere with planning a career based on the reality of your Success Factors (discussed in Chapter 4).

Myth: If you are frustrated at work, quit your job and find a new one.

Fact: Most people take their career problems from one job to the next. Don't be too anxious to leave your job, because the grass is rarely greener on the other side of the fence. Plan your next career step by focusing on your strengths and successes and not on your immediate problem. Then take action.

For example, if you find it difficult and frustrating working for your boss, you will be tempted to look for another job to eliminate the source of your problem. Experience proves that problems with the boss are rarely limited to basic personality conflicts. Instead of applying a hatchet solution or trying to psychoanalyze your boss or yourself, take a good look at successful experiences in your life where you have worked well with people, as well as the kind of people you have respected as superiors. Then plan your next step accordingly. Using the information in this book, you may even be able to rebuild your relationship with your boss.

Myth: The only way to find a job is to find a job opening or vacancy.

Fact: There are two other ways to get a job that, between them, are responsible for the majority of job offers: First, a job opening doesn't exist at the time of your interview with the company, but one occurs during the days or weeks following the interview. A qualified applicant already known to be available will have first consideration for that job. Second, a new job is created where there wasn't one before. This may be either an entirely new job category which fills an emerging need of a growing organization, or an addition to a group of jobs, such as another sales representative being added to an existing sales force.

Myth: You must have contacts to get a really good job.

Fact: Knowing how to *make* contacts will help you, not having contacts. Any contact you make on your own initiative, in your own occupational area or one closely related to it, will be far more valuable than a contact you inherit.

Myth: People are hired because they are qualified.

Fact: Far more people are hired because the interviewer liked them. Technical qualifications (specific experience, degrees, etc.) run a poor second. "If I like you, I may hire you; if I don't, I certainly won't."

This isn't as unfair as it sounds. None of us wants to work with someone we can't relate to. If you have genuine rapport with your prospective employer, his purpose and his work, you have a good chance of generating an offer. If not, you won't want the job and shouldn't want it. Unless you are desperate. And good career planning will eliminate the need to act out of desperation. You will always know what your next step is and will have laid the groundwork to take it at any time.

Myth: It's harder to find a good job if you are over forty.

Fact: If you have a career plan and you know how to look for a job, it's actually easier. And you will be increasingly qualified for better jobs as you become more experienced.

Yet, the over-forty myth is persistent, and the people who suffer most from it are the ones who believe it most. Every time someone over forty is observed having difficulty finding a job, people think: "Aha, this proves it," never really asking why the person is having a problem.

It is true that as you get older, employers are less willing to give you the benefit of the doubt and to assume that you can learn what you don't already know.

When you are forty years old (or, for that matter thirty or fifty), employers expect you to know who you are and where you are going. You are increasingly expected to know how to demonstrate your value to them.

No one will hire you, or refuse to hire you, on the basis of age alone. But with a career plan, and the ability to demonstrate years of achievements based on using your greatest talents and skills, you will become more valuable to prospective employers with each passing decade.

Myth: You have to be aggressive to get ahead.

Fact: Unless you are highly skilled in human relations, aggressiveness leads to offensiveness and long-term career decline. What you must be is *purposeful*. Having a life and career purpose attracts success. Having a purpose during a job interview makes a successful interview more likely.

Myth: A resume must be a complete chronological record of every job you have ever held.

Fact: Such resumes reflect lack of purpose. Once you have established a job and career objective, list only those facts that relate to your objective and support it. Resumes don't get jobs; people get jobs. A resume should reflect and support your purpose and nothing else.

Myth: If the resume is well written, its appearance is immaterial. Photocopies are okay.

Fact: The appearance of your resume says a lot about you. You wouldn't go to an interview wearing a T-shirt. A typeset or photocomposed resume is relatively inexpensive and tells the interviewer you think of yourself as a professional.

Myth: Placement agencies work for the job seeker.

Fact: Placement agencies help the employer find job applicants. They are responsible to the employer and are paid by the employer. In most states they are carefully controlled. Unethical agencies usually don't survive for very long in this competitive field. If you recognize and accept their purpose, you can profitably incorporate them in your total job search. The secret of success here is to cooperate with the agencies without turning over control of your job search and your career to them.

Myth: People are hired by personnel departments.

Fact: Personnel departments have many important functions, but they can only screen you, they can rarely hire you. You have not in any real sense applied for a job, or been considered for hiring, until you have talked with your prospective boss. Avoid application through personnel departments whenever possible and you will avoid being screened out in advance.

Myth: Interviews are controlled by the interviewer.

Fact: You control the interview. If you have a clear purpose in mind for the interview, you can take control of its direction while recognizing and responding to the interviewer's purpose. You will also earn his or her respect. Few passive interviewees will be considered for positions of responsibility.

Myth: The purpose of an interview is to get a job.

Fact: This is not true of most interviews. Here are some realistic purposes: to establish rapport with the interviewer; to get information from the interviewer; to give information to the interviewer; to be referred to others; to get a second interview; to get the offer of a job; and to negotiate working conditions and compensation.

If your purpose matches that of your interviewer, if both of you are on the same wavelength, and if both of you benefit, you will have only successful interviews. For instance, the first purpose of any interviewer who meets you for the first time will be to find out who you are. Interviewees commonly interfere with this purpose by attempting to sell themselves into a job about which, at this point, they know very little.

By recognizing the interviewer's purpose and matching it with your own, you have an opportunity to establish rapport on the human level, thereby creating a favorable climate for success.

Myth: The more advance research you do on an organization or an interviewer, the better.

Fact: One or two good questions asked during an interview are worth more than hours of advance research. You achieve two goals by asking questions *and listening to their answers*:

You get the information, and you establish rapport with the interviewer. Naturally it is useful to get some advance information in order to know what questions to ask. Would you rather be told by someone "I know all about you" or "I like what I heard about you; I'd like to know more"?

Myth: You are required to give both your salary history and your salary requirements when requested to do so.

Fact: Giving salary information to a prospective employer will always be to your disadvantage. You will be setting upper limits beyond which you will go only with great difficulty, if at all. For instance, if you give your current or expected salary level as $18,000, your future employer is unlikely to offer you $23,000, regardless of your actual value to him. In most cases, you will be unhappy with your income level sooner or later, which leads to resentment toward your employer. Both you and your employer will lose by this.

There are many methods to avoid giving this type of information without offending your interviewer. You will, in fact, earn your interviewer's respect.

Myth: If you have been turned down for a particular job by a particular individual in a company, you should eliminate that company from your job search.

Fact: Even though you were not hired for that job by that person at that time, it doesn't make sense to assume that no one in the entire company will consider you for any job ever again. On the contrary, if you have made a good impression and have established your credentials, you may have the inside track on a future position. You have every reason to stay in continuous contact with the organization. It is important not to allow your understandable feeling of rejection to lead you to reject the entire company. If the idea of working for them made sense in the past, it will continue to make sense in the future.

Myth: Once you are hired, you have a job.

Fact: What you have is an opportunity. What you do in the first day, the first week, and the first month determines whether or not you have a real job, a job that is part of a career, and what kind of a job it is.

Myth: You have to play politics to get ahead.

Fact: All career advancement is based on the ability to build constructive human relations, not game playing.

It is true that whenever two people are together in a room some form of politics takes place. There is no escaping it. But you have a choice of positive or negative politics. The building of constructive human relationships is a theme that you will find running through this book.

Myth: Academia and religion are havens from the rat race and from corporate politics.

Fact: The people-related nature of these fields makes them more, not less, susceptible to interpersonal problems than the so-called business world. On the other hand, for those with people-skills, there are great opportunities in these and related areas.

Myth: Contacts and resumes are relevant only when you are looking for a job.

Fact: It is much easier to make contacts while you are doing well in your job than when you are under the pressure of conducting a job search. And a resume should be a living document. It is a means of taking a periodic inventory of your career assets and should be updated at least once a year.

Myth: Your job is what your job description says it is. You have no control over it.

Fact: Job descriptions are a means to an end. They are statements of purpose, applicable for only short periods of time. Once a job description becomes a straitjacket, it must be changed.

Take the initiative to change it, with awareness of your employer's purpose and a commitment to helping him or her
achieve it.

Myth: Company policy is constant, unchangeable, and controls all
your activities on the job.

Fact: Company policy prevents chaos, but it is anything but rigid
at the top of the corporate pyramid. There is an ever-changing combination of problems and opportunities. Company
policy can be changed at the top, and it frequently is.

Take an active interest in the company's goals and purposes. That way, you can play an active part in bringing
about changes in the company's policies, in tune with those
goals and purposes, at whatever level within the company you
are.

Myth: An organizational diagram is a true reflection of the lines of
authority in an organization.

Fact: This is rarely true. An organizational structure depends
heavily on the interaction between people, and this usually
cannot be adequately represented in diagrammatic form.

One of the best ways to understand an organization is to
take a published organization diagram and, from your own
observations, draw in the real lines of power and information
flow.

Myth: It is up to the boss to offer a raise or promotion.

Fact: You can and must take the initiative. Most people feel that
there is something undignified about having to ask for recognition, that it should be freely offered.

Few employers are able to keep track of contributions
made by every employee, even with the greatest will in the
world. At best, they are aware in general terms only whether
an employee is doing well or not.

Bring your boss up to date on your work and your contributions. If this is done in the spirit of helping him or her arrive at a fair appraisal of your work, and a fair decision with regard to salary increases or promotions, it will be appreciated. If you don't take this initiative, you will sooner or later resent the lack of recognition, and a decline in your relationship with your boss will follow. You will eventually stop making contributions and will lose all chances for recognition.

Myth: The squeaky wheel gets the grease.
Fact: The "wheel" must be productive to merit the grease. What makes this myth so dangerous is that it appears, on the surface, to be borne out by observation.

You must be a productive contributor in order to earn recognition. Empty barrels make a lot of noise, but little attention is given to them. In any case, you are a person, not a wheel. And more effective means are available to you than impotent "squeaking." If you know you are pulling your weight, that you are doing a good job, use every means described in this book to communicate your value to your employer. The grease you get, in terms of tangible recognition, will lead to career advancement and career satisfaction. That is what your work is all about.

2
Ground Rules

Now that we have exposed some job and career myths, let's look at the reality of the work world. What is a good job? How does a job relate to a career? How do relationships with people affect both job and career?

The world *reality* is often used to label a particularly unpleasant fact or to serve as an excuse for declaring failure. So it is said that the reality of work or earning a living is a necessary evil. Enjoying your work is called a pleasant fantasy—but unrealistic. Company policy is called a reality. Your own view of what your job should be is said to be a dream, devoid of reality.

Carefully examine any statement made to you that is labeled "reality" or "being realistic." All too frequently these phrases camouflage the *user's* inability to cope with a problem.

You may be told that, "realistically speaking," there are no jobs in your field, despite the fact that thousands are working in such jobs. You may be told that, "realistically," high unemployment is a fact of life. It is said to be a "reality" that you can't get a good job without a degree, and so on.

Any of the facts described in this book are realities because they have been documented over the past thirty years by tens of thousands of our clients, and before that by the pioneers of job and career counseling. They have withstood the test of time and the fluctuations in the work world.

The next time you are being advised to be realistic, make sure this isn't a preface to being advised to accept failure.

There are three important realities of life that are expressed in the ground rules underlying every chapter of this book. Keep these ground rules in mind, and you will have no problem following everything that is written here.

The first ground rule: *A good job is a job you enjoy and a job in which you produce results. One without the other is insufficient.*

A job that results in nothing benefits no one other than yourself. And such a job ultimately will not benefit you, either, because everybody needs the feedback and recognition that come from achievements. Response and acknowledgment from others are required for true job satisfaction. On the other hand, results produced without enjoyment on your part soon turn sour and cause your attitude toward your job and your associates to deteriorate, thereby eliminating all chances for long-term job satisfaction.

You deserve to enjoy your work. If you don't, you are in trouble for a number of reasons. You spend a major part of your life in your job. Contrary to popular opinion, you can't build a fulfilling life around, or even next to, an unsatisfactory job. And there is danger in not enjoying a job; it will deteriorate and eventually disappear altogether.

You may feel that you can live with a job that isn't all you had hoped for but has some tangible rewards. One of the dangers of this assumption is that your dedication, creativity, ingenuity, and enjoyment will gradually shift to your non-job activities. You will begin merely to go through the motions. Your job performance will become mechanical, and you will stand still while the world moves on.

For a time you may not be aware of this, especially if you are skilled in the technical aspects of your work. One of the most frequent signals for job unhappiness is a physical or psychological symptom that doesn't seem to respond to normal treatment. Another is a deterioration in your relationship with your associates and superiors. This turns into hostility, and you will have lost the job in reality, even though you are still reporting to work every day.

The case of a fifty-three-year-old civil engineer illustrates this point. This man had been in charge of major construction projects in Europe and was now reduced to, in his own terms, fingering a pocket calculator at his desk. He was employed by one of the most prestigious engineering consulting firms in this country and had no intention of leaving the firm.

Although he was by nature a pleasant and gentle person, his associates found him abrasive, argumentative, and hostile, because of his job frustrations. His superiors did not consider using his considerable managerial experience, because they had every reason to believe no one in the firm would work for him.

A six-month project of rebuilding his relationship with his associates produced a promotion to project director. It was possible to rebuild the job and make it enjoyable and productive.

In another case, a different remedy had to be applied.

Our client was in the business of selling mechanical equipment to government institutions. He had always considered himself a good salesman and was doing well in his job. At the same time he was plagued by persistent backaches. He had seen doctors, had been X-rayed, and had done exercises. Nothing helped, and he continued to suffer. He started to have doubts about his work because he found the product he was selling uninspiring. He remembered taking a test in college that indicated a preference for creative design and for planning activities. He decided to seek career counseling and became our client.

As a result of re-evaluation of his basic interests and skills, together with the knowledge of his enjoyment of sales-related activities, he decided on a job change. He is now marketing manager of a major business systems firm. His new job allows him to use his planning and design interests to help his customers create business forms and systems that result in increased efficiency. After three months in the new job, his backaches disappeared.

By itself this example may not appear significant. But numerous cases of physical and psychological disorders, which range from headaches to hyperventilation and related problems and which disappeared after a career change, have convinced us that there is a direct connection.

The above examples have nothing to do with doing a good or bad job but with being in the right or wrong job. If you are in the right job for *you*, you will find yourself advancing in your career. The wrong job will cause a career decline as well as a deterioration of other aspects of your life.

This sounds straightforward. But there is a problem: A job sometimes looks right at the beginning, because it is new, exciting, and challenging. But it may still, for you, be the wrong job, and it will cause you to go into a personal and professional decline.

How do you know what job is right for you?

This question brings us to the second ground rule: *You can't have a career without having a job, and there is no job worth having that is not part of a career.*

In order to understand this statement, let's look at the words *job* and *career* more closely.

Webster defines a career as "a race—or running" and as "a specific course of action or occupation forming the object of one's life." Over the past twenty years, we have seen a gradual transformation in the meaning of the word *career*, from the first definition to the second one.

Now let's take a look at how Webster defines a *job*. Two definitions given are "a piece of work undertaken" and "a task, something that has to be done with great labor." I believe most people would add another definition: "A necessity of life, without which one cannot survive."

In fact, for most people, a job is a necessity. But you do have a choice. You can simply stumble from one "task" or "piece of work" into another, or you can embark on a "specific course of action, forming the object of your life"—a career.

Over the years, the concept of a career has undergone a strange metamorphosis. It was once thought to be merely a "slick" word—something that only advertising people and movie stars talked about. The only respectable career person was the "career diplomat." All others were considered part of an ulcer-producing rat race.

But in these enlightened times, people are beginning to realize that unhealthy tension is produced more by the 8-hour-a-day job you don't like than by the 12-hour-a-day career job you love.

Jobs are now advertised within the context of a career by many employers, from trucking firms to computer corporations. Universities are beginning to teach career planning. And the word *career* now connotes a positive purpose, rather than a rat race or a rut in which elderly civil servants get stuck.

If you take a closer look at what a career is, you will realize that there is no such thing as a career without a job. On the other hand, you can certainly have a job, or a series of jobs, without having a career.

In order to avoid having one job after another in a patchwork-quilt series of accidents, you must first recognize a purpose in your life's work.

This purpose is unique to each person. Without necessarily being aware of it, everyone builds a success pattern from childhood. Every time you did something particularly well, and derived satisfaction doing it, your ideal career pattern manifested itself. If you can remember and connect these events, or achievements, you are well on the way to identifying your career pattern. This process is one of the most reliable ways to start planning a career. And some of the most enlightened universities are now teaching this concept.

A career may well encompass several dramatic changes in your occupation. But there will always be a connecting thread, a continuous pattern of achievements, using the same talents and abilities. A good way to identify career growth is to look at the amount of satisfaction and personal fulfillment that goes with each job. And, usually, career growth parallels personal growth.

A job can be described as a combination of things you enjoy doing, things you don't mind doing, and things you dislike doing. You can take a reading on your career growth by making a list of the activities that fall into these three categories. If the number of tasks you enjoy completing keeps growing, and the tasks you are indifferent to or dislike keep diminishing, then you are on a course of action that represents genuine career advancement. If not, you are likely to be going down one of life's many dead-end streets.

Career consciousness is not limited to any age or sex. In fact, the older you get the easier it is to recognize genuine career patterns in yourself.

In a career there is always a Next Step. This may or may not include advancing your job with your present employer. Once you know your career patterns and you have career goals, you will always know the direction in which your Next Step will take you. The talents, skills, and abilities you will use in each job will be the ones you have always used, both in your career and in your total life. They will constantly be sharpened, and they will ensure that your career and all other aspects of your life will remain in tune with each other.

On the other hand, there are two common factors that can derail a career. They are misemployment and underemployment.

Misemployment is a job or a series of jobs that are built on talents and abilities other than the ones you have. You are *underemployed* in a job that may be right in principle, but it doesn't allow you to use your strengths to their fullest capacity. Both of those conditions are easily recognized when you know the strengths on which your career patterns and your career goals are built. You can then take action that will bring your career back on the track.

It should be understood that a job does not necessarily always mean paid employment. Volunteer activities can be very much part of a career because they can be fulfilling and productive. One of the most fulfilling and productive is the homemaker—male or female. The phrase "just a housewife," fortunately on its way out, has represented a monumental obstacle to the average person's understanding of the world of careers.

Here is an example that is typical of hundreds of clients who have sought our help over the years: A woman who had successfully presided over a large household for twenty-two years found herself with a decreasing challenge as her children grew up and became increasingly independent. She came to us and said that she had not been "working" for a long time and found the task of finding a job overwhelming. After all, she had "no recent experience" to offer.

She saw her work with her family and in her home as an interruption of her working life and wondered if it wasn't too late to start a career. She had even convinced her interviewers that she was not qualified for a job and had generated a number of rejections.

This client's problem was, of course, that she was out of touch with the part of the work world she was about to enter. She had no personal contacts in that world and no current knowledge of opportunities and requirements. In terms of proven abilities and tangible achievements, she was highly qualified for a number of challenging jobs. Once she recognized the combination of abilities that formed a very clear career pattern, including logistical and organizational ability together with rare skill in getting people to work together, it became a matter of presenting her qualifications in a businesslike way to the right people. She became the assistant personnel manager for a large department store.

By now you will have realized that there is a close connection between jobs and careers.

When searching for, finding, and carrying out a job, think in terms of your career purposes and goals. When planning a career, consider the jobs that are the building blocks of that career.

Throughout this book jobs *and* careers will be discussed together. Jobs will always be looked at in terms of the career of which they are a part, and careers will be discussed in terms of the jobs or activities of which they consist.

The third and *most important* ground rule underlying this book is the following: *The world of work is a world of people.*

There is no business organization without people. There is no company policy that isn't made by people. There is no such thing as management without people. People grant interviews, judge qualifications, make offers of employment.

An understanding of how people function is essential if you are to move successfully in the job and career world.

You do not need to be a trained psychologist to develop this knowledge. One simple fact, if understood and remembered, will lead you safely through the mass of human relationships in the job and career world: Business decisions, like all human decisions, are made partially on the rational and partially on the emotional level.

The rational or factual side of a statement or decision is usually communicated adequately in words. It remains for us to understand something about the role the emotions play, our own emotions as well as those of the people around us.

Job interviews provide good examples for this. You will rarely be made a job offer based solely on your technical qualifications for a job. If the interviewer doesn't accept you on the emotional level, if he or she doesn't like you, you will not receive an offer. On the other hand, if you have established personal rapport with an interviewer, you may often be chosen over someone with twice your qualifications. We see examples of this every day.

There should be nothing frightening or negative about this realization. The business world becomes much more accessible to you when you think of it as a world of people.

A young client, Harold G., decided that he wanted to become a salesman. He had been outstandingly successful in persuading people to his point of view in selling ideas, but he had never been paid for it. He had been trained as an engineer. No company would ever hire him as a salesman. But he knew that companies don't hire, people do.

So Harold wrote a resume that presented his job objective and qualifications in terms of his actual achievements rather than his past job descriptions, and he set out to make contact with people at the decision-making level. Not surprising, given Harold's ability to communicate, he persuaded the president of a small manufacturing firm that made the type of electrical equipment with which he was familiar to employ him as a sales engineer on a trial basis. The president not only was impressed by his strength of purpose, but had also taken a liking to him. Twelve years later Harold G. continues to enjoy a successful marketing career.

Being knowledgeable about and in command of our own emotions is just as important as being qualified in other ways. What do you do when an interviewer says to you: "But we are looking for a younger person!" Do you feel that you have been disqualified for the job? Do you walk away from your interviewer, or do you explain why your experience and ability make you more valuable for the job?

A few well-chosen questions would elicit the reason for the interviewer's preference for a younger person. You can then provide information to reassure your interviewer that your greater age is an asset to the company and not a drawback.

Our emotions frequently lead us to confuse objections with rejections. In reality they often turn out to be opportunities for clearing away confusion and prejudice. Statements such as: "We have never hired a woman for this position," "We were looking for someone with a master's degree," "You have only three years' experience in this field," allow you to demonstrate why these objections do not present obstacles to job performance. Frequently you can even suggest how a seeming disadvantage can be turned into an advantage.

One of our clients persuaded a prospective employer that the lack of an advanced degree would put him more on a level of rapport with the people under him, none of whom had academic training. His experience otherwise qualified him for the job, and he was hired, even though all his competitors for the job had academic certification.

In most cases objections about your being qualified for a job turn out to be simple requests for information and reassurance. By recognizing this you can turn objections into opportunities.

Sometimes "corporate policy" is given as the reason certain

qualifications are required. Corporate policy is created to prevent chaos in an organization. But in any sound business organization, corporate policy is responsive to changes and opportunities within as well as outside the company, and any organization that adheres to a rigid, inflexible set of policies does not survive for very long.

Recently a client who applied for a job to a well-known organization in the communications field was told at her first interview that the company hired "only from within." This statement is frequently made by interviewers and reflects a desire rather than a fact. As a morale-building policy, even when observed only partially, it is a valuable management tool.

Our client asked the interviewer if anyone with her exact qualifications was currently in the company's employ and available for the job. The answer was no; corporate policy was quietly shelved, and the interview proceeded without further objections. It was concluded successfully.

The organizational diagram is another good example of the "human" nature of the corporate world. Few such charts (or totem poles) reflect the actual lines of power or of communications. Organizations are people, and people cannot be reduced to diagrams. One of the first tasks of any Haldane client, on starting in a new job, is to study the real relationships between people around him or her, as compared to the lines of authority established by the company.

Throughout this book, human relations are discussed as an integral part of job and career building.

The emotional aspect of human relationships sometimes becomes difficult to handle in negative job and career situations. This will be discussed in the following chapter. However, there is no intent here to portray emotions by themselves as a negative force. On the contrary, with an understanding of the role of the emotions comes the ability to benefit from their proper functioning. The emotions provide the energy for all great achievement. Knowledge of your own and others' emotional responses will enable you to turn problems into opportunities and to take control of your job and your career.

Knowledge of your emotional responses is particularly important when you are faced with job and career problems, the subject of Chapter 3.

3
How to Solve Job and Career Problems

In the first stages of seasickness, you are afraid you will die. Later you are afraid you *won't* die.

The same is true of a job you don't like: At first you are afraid of losing the job; later you realize that it may be even worse to keep it.

In this chapter I'll discuss two categories of employment problems: First, the trauma created by being terminated together with the resulting unemployment problems, and second, the problems of being unhappy with the job you have. I will also demonstrate an effective method of dealing with job and career problems that was first developed by Bernard Haldane and differs in some important respects from the traditional approach to identifying and solving problems.

When a person is terminated, the first reaction is emotional. A rational understanding of the event usually follows much later, but in some cases, it is blocked from ever happening. Because your reactions take place at the emotional level, without much reasoned control, they can be dangerous to you.

Here are some typical examples of negative emotional responses to being fired.

- Telling the boss off. This may make you feel better, but it can create a number of negative trends that you may find hard to control later, especially if you stay in the same career field.

- Stopping off for one or more drinks on the way home. This is a more common reaction than is generally realized. When in the twin grip of anger and alcohol, disastrous decisions are often made.

- Going on vacation in order to forget about the whole unpleasant event. In the first place, it doesn't work, and in the second, it will increase the amount of inertia you will have to overcome when you finally start your search for the next job. If you feel you deserve a vacation, the best time to take it is after you have accepted a job offer and before you report to work. This is usually possible, and such a vacation has great benefits, not the least of which is that you start your next job with a clear and refreshed mind.

- A variation on the "going-on-vacation" theme is sitting in front of the television set at home. Severance pay can be both a help and a hindrance, depending on your use of it. Severance pay can finance part or all of your job search, or it can simply help you to put off the inevitable Next Step and add to the mountain of inertia in your path to the next job.

You may be led by a negative emotion to make some understandable but wrong assumptions. One is that your family and friends will despise you for losing your job; you will be considered worthless. You may feel that everyone is looking at you as you walk down the street, as if your misfortune has suddenly become visible to the whole world. You may fear that being out of work means you probably won't get another job.

The fact is that most people have been fired at one time or another. You are not alone. If having been fired meant not being able to find another job, most of the population of this country would be permanently out of work. Many of your friends have been in the situation you are now facing.

One assumption you can safely make is that no one will offer you a job while you feel and look like a walking disaster area. Employers don't hire problems, they hire people to solve problems.

So the Next Step is to take positive action. Start by enlisting the support of your family and closest friends by including them in your planning. They will respond with enthusiasm. Finding a good position is a full-time job that requires all the ingenuity and stamina you can muster. The time to begin is at 9:00 A.M. the next day.

To counteract feeling worthless, take stock of your assets. They are illustrated in your achievements, both on and off the job. Write down as many of your accomplishments as you can remember, but list at least ten. An achievement is anything that you did well, enjoyed doing, and were proud of doing.

This is not an idle ego-building exercise. Select specific events, not general abilities; write them down in detail and include results. When you have finished, study what you have written. Underline activities and results that occur in more than one achievement. Soon you will find a pattern of skills or talents. If not, add more achievements, even relatively minor ones, until you start seeing repeated successful actions emerging. If you find this difficult, ask someone close to help.

The following are two examples of achievements from one of our clients:

1. Five years ago I enlisted the help of my staff in reorganizing a complex filing system for my company. We relabeled all folders and created an easy-to-read index. As a result, the time it takes to find a document has been cut in half, and no document has been lost since then. The filing system is still in use today.

2. All members of my family enjoy reading. Our home is full

of books, but, until recently, specific books took a long time to find, and some books seemed lost altogether. So I built new bookshelves. I then sorted all our books into categories, labeled the bookshelves, and got my family to learn how the system worked and to return all books to their proper places. Since then books have been easy to find, and I received many compliments from friends and neighbors on my system.

It is easy to see that these two examples begin to indicate a pattern. This person took pride in bringing order into disorganized situations and in creating systems. An ability to get other people involved is also implied.

Once an ability pattern or success pattern emerges, it can be reinforced by many other examples. The more examples you find, the more certain you can be that the ability, skill, or talent indicated is a genuine strength and should be part of any job you hold in the future. It should be a strong factor in your entire career.

The Next Step is to write a resume or to revise the resume you already have. Make sure that the skills and talents you identified in your achievement analysis are reflected in your resume. Some of the achievements you write down may be stronger than the job description listed on your present resume and should be included in the revised version.

If you are not sure what your next job should look like, it will be important to read Chapter 4, "Setting Objectives," before you rewrite your resume. You will spend at least a whole day and maybe more to accomplish the above. But you will now have a realistic objective and the documentation as well as the confidence to back it up.

If you are under financial pressure, deal with that next, so you don't have to look over your shoulder constantly and worry about paying bills. For major debts, such as a mortgage or a large loan, visit the manager of your bank. When you explain

your situation openly, together with your plans for dealing
with it, your bank manager can often help you make a temporary arrangement to ease your burden. The manager now has
a personal stake in the success of your job search. Also, as you
know, bankers are good contacts to have in the community.

Most people to whom you owe money will accept a good-
will gesture, such as a token payment, sometimes as little as
one dollar, together with a written explanation of your situation and a commitment to resume full payments on acceptance of a job.

If you are under heavy financial pressure, you may need to
consider a temporary or part-time job. Experience shows that
a 25 percent reduction in your salary expectations can more
than double your employment opportunities. Such a job has
two advantages: It allows you to look for a good job from a
position of being employed, which will give you added confidence. And it reduces the loss of income considerably. For the
latter reason Bernard Haldane has called it a "Stop-Loss Job."

There are two types of Stop-Loss Jobs. The first is a job in
your career field, but at a lower level. The second is a job in
an unrelated field that requires little skill or experience, and is
relatively easy to find. The virtue of this kind of Stop-Loss Job
is that it may have flexible hours, thus allowing you to use
prime daytime hours for interviewing. Depending on your in-
clinations, these jobs can include selling a product or service,
working in a retail establishment, or driving a taxi.

As a last resort or desperation measure, Stop-Loss Jobs may
be damaging to your self-respect, but as part of a purposeful
approach to bridging a career gap, they will have no negative
emotional implications.

Is it fair to the employer to enter into a temporary relationship with the intention of leaving as soon as a better opportunity arises?

The answer is twofold: First, seen from that point of view,

all jobs are temporary; and for many of our clients, the Stop-Loss Job turned into a good career position through rapid on-the-job advancement, once they were able to prove themselves. Second, as long as you carry out your job to the best of your ability, you are meeting your obligation to your employer. Once the job no longer meets your requirements, or those of the employer, it should come to an end in any case.

Some people become worried about how a position of short duration, at reduced responsibility and income, affects their overall work record or career progress. In Chapter 7, "Building Communications," I will show how to present your employment history.

The case of a fifty-one-year-old man who was terminated unexpectedly illustrates many of the points discussed so far in this chapter.

I was completely unprepared when my boss told me that my job was being eliminated. I was too stunned to react. I don't remember what I said to my boss. Among the thoughts that passed through my mind, the one I remember most was: "How am I going to tell my wife about this?"

I remember dimly that someone told me that stopping for a drink on the way home after being fired was a no-no. I'm not even sure I would have been able to get it down if I had tried.

One of my assumptions was shattered when I presented the bad news to my family. My wife, refusing to collapse from the shock, reminded me that the life we had together was built on something stronger than the permanence of my job.

So we decided to start at 9:00 A.M. on the dot the next morning to make plans for my becoming re-employed, before I had a chance to start feeling sorry for myself.

The first problem I needed to deal with was the feeling that everyone was looking at me. I thought of buying a new suit (which I couldn't afford) and of all the things I had read about that would improve my appearance and make me look younger, such as dying my hair.

My wife came to the rescue again, reminding me that my suit and gray hair had not been a problem before. The difference was that the satisfaction of having done a day's work would be missing now. But why should it?

I had read somewhere that finding a job was the most difficult of all jobs. There ought to be lots of opportunity for doing a good day's work. Right there my wife and I decided on a 9 to 5 schedule with plenty of opportunity for overtime. We also decided on taking our weekends, or at least Sundays seriously by doing the less expensive things we most enjoyed as a family.

We also made a point not to avoid people. We decided to talk openly with our friends about my situation and feelings. We have been told by many of our acquaintances since then that they were inspired by our attitude.

The next thing we had to tackle was the one most likely to cause fear. The subject of money. Despite my chronic disinclination to budget, I actually enjoyed the project of taking stock of our financial resources, cash and otherwise.

We dealt with the more difficult subject of debts in the following way: Every one of the people we owed payments to received a letter explaining my problem, and containing both a small token payment and a promise to bring the account current as soon as I was employed again.

The biggest obligation was the mortgage on our house. I made an appointment with the manager of the local branch of my bank. I must say that I learned more about the good side of human nature during that period than in all the time I was gainfully employed.

Our Next Step was the organizing of a job search. Here I hit a snag: The culture we are living in considers being unemployed as some sort of disease. Although I felt my attitude was positive,

I also know that in my profession available jobs were known to be scarce, and competition was intense.

To be realistic I had to consider the possibility of a six- to ten-month period of unemployment, and I felt that my resources, as well as the patience of my creditors, would not stretch that far. I had heard that the availability of jobs doubled with a one-quarter decrease in salary expectations.

So my wife and I set an arbitrary period of six weeks of concentrated job search before deciding to settle for a temporary, lower-level job in order to stop or reduce the loss of income.

Just as we were about to start on the latest crop of newspapers, it occurred to me that I now had a unique opportunity to make a mid-career adjustment in my professional activity.

Although I had, by and large, enjoyed what I was doing, my job had been mostly administrative in character. Those ideas that I was able to contribute to the improvement in our firm's product were considered to be outside my normal duties and had not been rewarded financially. Yet there had been many such instances, and I decided to include them in my resume.

As we were preparing a new resume, my wife and I became quite anxious to get a reaction from a few friends to my expanded job objective. At first some of them doubted the wisdom of changing my objective during a period of unemployment. But when they heard me talk about it, they agreed that my apparently increased sense of self-worth would be a point in my favor during the coming interviews.

The four productive days spent bringing our finances in order and making job-plan decisions not only resulted in a resume I could feel good about, but generated a sense of satisfaction in me that had been absent in my work for some time.

I believe many of my interviewers were favorably impressed with my attitude. In the end, one of the first people I had seen called me some weeks later to tell me about an opportunity he had heard about. This resulted in an interview and eventually in a job offer that I accepted under favorable conditions.

As a result of this experience, I have made a few resolutions that I am determined to keep:

"I will never again be caught by surprise by an unforeseen development in my company.

"If I see a change taking place, I will stay in close communication with my employer so I have an opportunity to adapt myself to the change.

"I will set aside a certain amount of money as an insurance policy against similar occurrences.

"Every person who gave me advice, counsel, or help in any way during my job search will receive a letter of thanks, if it takes me and my family a week to type them all.

"I will take my family to a big dinner at an expensive restaurant on my first paycheck, and you may call me a spendthrift."

There are ways to prevent job loss or at least to recognize it before it happens. This may be cold comfort to you once you have lost your job. But the negative emotional reaction to being fired or terminated from a job is such a crucial factor, the recognition that this need never happen to you again is very important in retaining your emotional equilibrium.

There are recognizable signs of an impending job loss, regardless of whether this loss is brought on by your own actions (or inactions) or whether it is the result of an organizational change.

A "phase-out" is in progress when you are being assigned less important duties or projects or when nobody seems to care whether or not you are doing a good job. A gradual or abrupt deterioration of your relationship with your superiors can be a sign of an impending change in your employment status. Here, be aware that angry encounters and confrontations with your boss mean, in almost every case, that you still have an opportunity to turn the negative trend around. However, once you are treated with cold politeness or your superior's anger has turned into indifference, you may have been written off. Termination may be only a matter of timing.

Reading these signs early gives you an opportunity to plan appropriate action, such as getting on the boss's wavelength and, with his or her help, curing the problem—or getting some lifeboats over the side and exploring other job opportunities.

In a case where the impending termination is caused by organizational change or other circumstances beyond your control, there are signs you can read far ahead of time. The organizational grapevine is frequently a good indicator that a change is about to take place, but it is an unreliable guide to the nature and timing of that change. Whether the change is a shrinkage of the organization, a phasing out of your job or department, impending bankruptcy, or a planned merger with or acquisition by another company, key people in your organization are involved in the decision-making process and possess accurate information.

Get access to this information. Spend part of your time communicating with people at the decision-making level. Communication has to be established early. Once your need is acute, it is usually too late to start the process.

By reading the signs, and reading them accurately, you can take action while you are still in control of your situation.

But watch out! Your emotions may play tricks on you at this point. You may develop occupational paranoia and interpret every event as an impending disaster. This can take the form of a self-fulfilling prophecy and, by way of an increasingly negative attitude toward your employer, bring about the event you fear.

It is also possible to avoid looking at the facts and living in hope that the disaster will be averted or doesn't exist. Your reasoning will then turn into rationalization, and you will engage in wishful thinking.

Although unexpected termination presents a person with stark choices, one of the most insidious job problems is the gradual deterioration and disintegration of a job over a period of time. You haven't actually been fired. You may even have considerable "job security." But in any real sense you have lost the job, and you might as well face it. Early symptoms of such job deterioration are boredom, stagnation, and a gradual worsening of your day-to-day relationship with your superiors and associates. Often a feeling of being used or exploited signifies that you have lost control in your job.

The causes for such trends are either situational or occupational. A situational problem is one that arises because you are either at the wrong level in your organization, in the wrong environment, performing the wrong duties, or working under or with the wrong people. Wrong for you, that is. A purely situational job problem has nothing to do with career field; the problem can be solved by making an adjustment in your current job situation. Sometimes you can even make this adjustment without changing employers.

A few years ago a client with a background in publishing and a talent for book design told us that she had lost the support of the vice-president to whom she reported. She was no longer invited to meetings, and hostile encounters with others in the company were daily occurrences. She made the assumption that she was being discriminated against as a woman—all of the other executives in the company were men.

An analysis of this client's skills, talents, and motivation confirmed her belief that she was in the right career. But a situational analysis also showed that, over the years, she had delegated all the activities she enjoyed and kept only administrative and supervisory functions, which had nothing to do with her original choice of publishing as a career. Her attitude toward her associates had gradually soured, and she had become known as a person to avoid. Once she identified the problem, she took action. With the cooperation of her superiors, who breathed a sigh of relief, she rewrote her own job description, hired an administrative assistant, took over direct design responsibility once more, and began to enjoy her work again.

This is an example of a *situational* job problem. However, the analysis might have shown that this client was in the wrong field altogether. In that case, any attempt to rebuild her present job would not have dealt with the real issue.

When an *occupational* problem exists (when you are in the wrong career), career *change* is the only realistic response. In a large or diversified organization, it is sometimes possible to manage a career change without changing employers. But in the majority of cases, a career change requires a change in employers. In some cases this may be a drastic change to an entirely new sector of the work world, or even to self-employment.

The difficulty comes when assumptions are made without a thorough analysis of the job problem. One of these assumptions is that a change of jobs will automatically eliminate the problem, whatever it is. "The grass is always greener . . ." etc. It is quite possible for you to take your job or career problem with you from one job to another and never solve it.

We had a client who had what he called an authority problem. He would start every job well, but soon a split would develop between him and his superior, leading to eventual resignation or termination. It turned out that the client was in the wrong career, one that did not allow him to use his obvious talents. It is natural for all of us to blame people when we have a problem we can neither recognize nor solve. So our client developed hostility to his bosses in all his jobs, blaming them for assigning work he didn't enjoy and apparently ignoring his real talents. Application of "cocktail-hour psychology" allowed him to label his difficulty as an authority problem and file it away, while continuing to suffer.

The first step in identifying and solving a work problem, whether it is a short-term job problem or a long-term career problem, is to clearly identify the personal pattern of skills, talents, and abilities you most enjoy using and from which you get satisfaction and results.

Each job consists of combinations of duties and functions, some of which you enjoy and some of which you don't. The real definition of job and career advancement is to maximize the duties you enjoy carrying out and to minimize the others. You will usually be able to enlist the help and support of your employers, because most employers know that productivity is related directly to job enjoyment and motivation. Only a motivated employee can be productive. Any employer or boss who does not realize this represents a job problem for you and cannot be too actively avoided.

Not every human relations problem is the symptom of a deeper cause. There are genuine incompatibilities between people, and there are bosses and associates who are negative and hostile for reasons not connected with you or your work. However, most people are too quick to assign blame for a poor relationship to the other person. Many people come to us with the statements "My boss is . . . incompetent . . . dishonest . . . hostile . . . using me . . . out to get me . . . irrational . . . etc." In most cases it turns out that both employer and employee have contributed to the interpersonal relations problem.

If you have such a problem, and you take the initiative, you will find that it is possible to rebuild most relationships. In Chapter 13 you will find step-by-step instructions for doing this.

But the ability to solve your work problems, and the absence of such problems, does not automatically guarantee career satisfaction.

Genuine motivation can come only from within you; from the knowledge that your work is right for you, that it allows you to use your greatest personal assets, and that you get everyday satisfaction and fulfillment from doing your job. If those conditions are not met, no amount of motivational incentives provided by your employer will make you either happy or productive.

If you have decided that your problem should be solved by a career change, then identifying your greatest strengths, talents, and skills will pay dividends.

Your talents and skills are the bridge between your old career and the new one. Any set of talents and skills that you have used to produce satisfaction and results in the past will document your potential for success when recombined and used in a new career field or environment. This method is often called "transfer of skills."

In this chapter I have referred to a method for solving job and career problems that differs from the traditional approach to problem solving.

Traditionally you are told that you must first identify a problem before you can develop a solution and implement it. But because of your emotional involvement in your job and career problems, the traditional method is not productive and wastes valuable energy while you turn a problem over and over in your mind.

Instead, when you become aware of a job or career problem, start by identifying your assets, your greatest strengths, *not your problems.*

Only after you have clearly identified your personal assets—your arsenal of strengths, abilities, skills, and talents——should you look at your current problem, analyze it, and deal with it in the light of the positive self-knowledge you have gained. To put it succinctly: Strengths *before* weaknesses. Or: Positive *before* negative.

If you have any of the job and career problems described in this chapter, do the following:

When you are unhappy in your work, find out in what working situations you function best, then take action to bring about the ideal conditions by whatever means are available to you. Don't let your emotional reaction to your current problem dictate your next career step.

In the case of a job loss, first become aware of your assets and plan your Next Step accordingly. *Then* analyze the events that led to the loss of your job. The first step will tell you what to do, the second what to avoid in the future. Both steps are important, but they must be taken in the order described.

Developing your strengths will give you the confidence to deal with your problems or weaknesses. It will also create in you the ability to see problems in terms of opportunities, which is surely the hallmark of all successful and dynamic people.

4
Setting Objectives

Observe any dynamic and successful person and you will recognize that he or she has a sincere, deep, conscious commitment to a purpose. An activity without purpose leads nowhere. It is meaningless. In the job and career world, setting an objective is the same as establishing a purpose.

How do you establish a job and career purpose?

Start by knowing yourself. In this chapter I will discuss the meaning of objectives and how to achieve the self-knowledge needed for setting imaginative objectives. You will learn a step-by-step process for developing job and career objectives for yourself as well as a method to gain the insight into the work world that makes these objectives realistic.

First, a few words about "success." What is it; how do you define it; how do you recognize it?

For the purposes of this book, success is the positive outcome, or result, of a plan or an action—your plan, your action, not someone else's.

Given this definition, success comes in many shapes and sizes. A two-minute conversation can be successful. A career or even a whole life can be successful. The definition is yours. If the outcome of an activity or effort is what you wanted it to be, it is a success!

An effort cannot be successful if there was no purpose; however, the purpose may not have been conscious. The more you become conscious of your purposes, or have objectives, the more you will be in control of your successes.

Guard against allowing other people or society to decide what your criteria for success should be! In many ways your definition may be conditioned by the community in which you live. Make sure you have examined your own criteria carefully.

In our society there is a heavy pressure on young people to "know what they want to do." Yet very little attention is given to the means they can use to *plan* a career. There is also a humorous saying used by older people: "Someday I'll find out what I want to do with my life." Both phrases illustrate that our society has very little understanding of career planning.

It's okay not to know what you want to do for the rest of your life. It's okay not to have a scenario for your life and work. In fact, such decisions at too early a stage in your life are likely to have the effect described in the joke about a mind like a cement mixer: all mixed up and set in concrete.

What is important to building a successful career is the knowledge of the basic *components*, or *building blocks*, of that career. If you know what these components are and use them, you will have a successful career. If you don't, you probably won't.

Sometimes we hear objectives referred to as job or career objectives. There is in fact very little difference between the two concepts. A job objective describes the immediate Next Step in your career, and the career objective applies to future career steps. But a job objective and a career objective must always be in tune with each other. Your job objective is realistic only if it takes into account your long-term career goals, and a career objective makes sense only if each job on your career path contains the same ingredients as your career objective.

For example, if the basic building blocks of your career include writing ability, a liking and aptitude for detail, and an understanding of mechanical and engineering principles, you might choose technical writing as an early job objective. Your long-term career objective choices might include heading up a firm of technical writers, becoming a design engineer, or anything else that uses these building blocks, as well as others that will be identified as you advance in your profession.

From this example you can see that, while both job objectives and career objectives share the same basic components (writing, detail, mechanical/engineering aptitude), the job objective describes the immediate job goal based on currently identified and available abilities. A career objective, however, is constantly in a state of flux. New information and insight are used to reshape the career objective, without ever changing its basic components, but adding new ones as they are identified, and sometimes changing the emphasis from one component to another. In the above example, the emphasis might change from writing to designing, or to supervising writers or designers.

A perennial problem in career planning is the decision about whether or not to pursue a college education or other plan of study. General answers don't satisfy this problem. If your purpose is to develop and use skills that cannot be found as part of a formal course of study, the answer is not to use valuable energy to study subjects that are irrelevant to your career purposes. On the other hand, if academic knowledge, recognition, or certification are part of your career plans, a program of study tailored as closely as possible to your career purposes is a reasonable plan. Once you have gone through the process described later in this chapter, you will be in a position to make a valid career-oriented decision.

One of the most common perceived obstacles to job and career planning is expressed in the statements "I don't know what's out there," or "I don't know what jobs I fit into," or even "I don't know what jobs are available." All of these objections are either premature or irrelevant. It isn't a question of what's out there but of what's in you. Before any information about the job market is useful to you, you must get to know yourself better.

Once you understand the ingredients of a successful and fulfilling career for yourself, you can start the task of building a bridge to the world of jobs. Your career building blocks are the girders of that bridge. To pursue this word picture further: You have started on the near bank of the river, using what you know about your own skills, abilities, and interests. You may have only a hazy view of what is on the other side (the job market). As you identify the building blocks of your future career, you extend the superstructure of your bridge, and you start to approach the other side. Once you know where you are heading, you will be able to build pylons on the other shore: your contacts in the work world.

The development of job and career objectives is a continuous process. Each day, month, and year you know more about yourself. At the same time you deepen and broaden your knowledge of the world of work. You will continue to refine your career objectives and to add to them. Your purposes will become stronger and better defined. This will have a visible effect on your entire life-style and your personality.

There is only one impediment to this process: the setting of arbitrary end-goals, the casting-in-concrete of final life and career goals. The pursuit of a career should be a *continuous* adventure. We have worked with clients in their sixties and seventies who were embarked on career adventures that gave them a zest for life, making them the equals in spiritual, mental, and physical fitness of people half their age.

George M. was seventy-one years old when he became our client. He was a minister in a small suburban community. For years he had detested what he called "infighting" among various members of his congregation. He felt he was always caught in the middle. It was difficult for him to face the fact that he had never really liked dealing directly with people and that he had no talent for handling situations of conflict and confrontation between people.

He had always secretly longed to participate in the building of a church. His avocation consisted of architectural studies, and he had accumulated a vast collection of architectural photographs of cathedrals and churches all through Europe and the United States.

Within a few months of his becoming our client, he had delegated his ministry to someone else and had become involved in a project to construct a new church in a neighboring community.

Although he had not studied architecture formally, he had a considerable knowledge of the process of planning and constructing a building, combined with financial and administrative ability. Soon he was totally involved in the construction effort, beginning with supervising a successful fund-raising campaign. He also assisted in choosing the decor, including the stained-glass windows. George told me that it was well worth waiting seventy-one years for a satisfying and successful career. All the things he really liked doing finally culminated in this spectacular achievement.

This is only one example out of many that prove there is no such thing as too late!

The setting of rigid goals is usually exemplified by statements such as these: "By the time I am forty, I intend to be president of my own company," or "I have set a goal of earning $40,000 by age thirty." For most people such goal setting is very destructive. As with everything else, however, there are exceptions to this rule. If you know yourself very well and have a realistic view of your career goals, such an objective may be an achievable purpose for you. In any case, it is possible to have a strong career objective without having a rigid end-goal in mind.

We now come to the actual process of setting up a job and career objective. It is advisable to set aside many hours or, better yet, several days for this task. For some people the completion of this process will produce entirely new, sometimes surprising insights. For others it will give structure to something of which they had already been aware.

The sequence of steps in this procedure is important, and none of the steps should be omitted. You will get out of it what you put into it; no more, no less. The effort and thought applied will result in insight gained.

Objectivity is not required at this stage. It won't produce self-knowledge. Whatever information you produce will, at a later stage, be tested against objective reality. In other words, there is plenty of time to be realistic later. Start by allowing your imagination and your feelings to be part of this process.

Setting job and career objectives begins with *Success Factor Analysis*. A Success Factor is an activity, an ability, skill or talent used in an achievement. The analysis of Success Factors was developed by Bernard Haldane many years ago and has been used for decades by thousands of people and organizations throughout the world. It is one of the few methods of developing information that realistically incorporates thought, imagination, and emotions into a process of self-assessment.

The accuracy of Success Factor Analysis has never been approached by any other method, even the most sophisticated psychological tests available to modern behavioral science. Countless successful careers have been built on the use of this method. In other words, it works.

There are nine steps in developing your job and career objectives.

Step One. Start the process by writing down ten to fifteen specific achievements from every phase of your life (childhood to present; work, leisure, school, military service, etc.). There must be at least ten achievements.

An achievement is anything that you enjoyed doing and that gave you a feeling of accomplishment. Recognition by others may or may not have been a factor, but it is not essential at this point. The achievement must be a specific event or action, and it must have been viewed by you as successful. General descriptions of skills, abilities, and repeated successes are not part of this step.

Put each of these achievements on a separate page. Describe the event in detail. Go back and add more details if they occur to you later.

As a guideline to follow, describe what you did, how you did it, and what the outcome or result was.

Keep reviewing important periods of your life as well as key events to determine if there are any achievements you have overlooked. For the purpose of this analysis, small events like learning to ride a bicycle are equivalent to big ones like saving a life or masterminding a successful corporate merger.

Here are examples from two different clients:

> At the request of our company's president, I supervised the move of the company to new premises. I talked with each department head to find out his needs for keeping his employees productive during the period of upheaval caused by the move. I also coordinated the movers with electricians, carpenters, and telephone people so that we would have a minimum of downtime during the move. I had to decide whether it was better to make the move on a weekend to avoid lost production, or whether the cost of the workers' overtime would wipe out the weekend moving advantage. With the help of the controller, I performed a financial analysis and decided to start the move on a Friday afternoon. I supervised the move very closely, staying on the new premises and serving as a liaison between the var-

ious groups of people involved. As a result, the move was completed in record time at less than the estimated expense and with a minimum of downtime in company operations.

In June, I planned a party at my apartment. I talked my roommates into helping me. We decided on the menu, designed place cards, and I did all the shopping. My older roommate is a good cook, so I asked her to prepare the food. I wrote all the invitations and set the table together with my other roommate. At the last minute, I found out that the cream I bought had turned sour. So I asked my friends to perform introductions and slipped out to buy a new carton of cream. During the party, two of the guests got into a hostile argument, but I was able to calm them down and, by changing the subject, helped them to become friendly with each other again. The party was a success, and I received many phone calls and thank-you notes afterward.

Step Two. Identify as many Success Factors as you can find in each achievement.

Grammar is not important at this stage. You can express Success Factors as nouns, verbs, or anything else. The ability to organize, for instance, can be expressed as "organizational ability," "organizing," or "organize." What is important is that the word refers to something clearly involved in making the achievement happen. It is not necessary, at this point, to be concerned about whether or not any Success Factor contained in an achievement refers to an ever-present talent or occurred just in this one instance.

The two examples of achievements given above contain the following Success Factors:

First example:
    Supervising (I supervised . . .)
    Communicating (I talked with each department
      head . . .)

Liaison

Planning/Organizing/Coordinating (I made appointments with . . . , etc.)

Analysis (I performed a financial analysis)

Decision Making

In addition to the above Success Factors, there are a number of "qualitative" Success Factors, such as attention to detail and resourcefulness. They are contained in both achievements.

Second example:

Planning (I planned the party . . . .)

Organizing

Persuading (I talked my roommates into . . .)

Deciding (We decided on a menu . . .)

Delegating (I asked her to do all the cooking, . . . I asked my friends to perform introductions . . .)

Cooperating (I set the table together with . . .)

Problem Solving (The cream had turned sour, etc.)

Human Relations (I helped . . . calm an argument . . .)

Art/Design (I designed place cards)

With more detail, the achievement might have yielded additional Success Factors, such as showmanship or performance under pressure. But by themselves these Success Factors don't say anything about you yet. They refer only to the achievement being analyzed.

The strength of this approach is that it is not scientific or objective in a limited sense. Instead, it encourages you to be subjective. Any inaccuracies or omissions at this stage will be automatically corrected at later stages.

Two people can list similar Success Factors, but the words may have a totally different meaning for each of them. Creative imagination in one person may be used in quite a different context from that of another person.

Although the number of possible Success Factors is virtually unlimited, we have found that there are a number of Success Factors that appear in most people's achievements, although in different combinations. Here is a list of those factors:

Human relations, interpersonal relations, people.

Managing, leading, supervising, decision making.

Communicating, persuading, selling, teaching, counseling, writing, public speaking, acting, performing, mediating.

Planning, organizing, coordinating.

Creating, artistic, imagination, inventing, designing.

Research, analysis, observing.

Problem solving, troubleshooting.

Technical, mechanical, scientific.

Calculating, numbers, finance, cost control, cost/profit awareness.

Here are the most common qualitative Success Factors, which are often overlooked:

Ingenuity, resourcefulness.

Commitment, dedication.

Initiative, independence.

Perseverance, drive.

Start your Success Factor Analysis by reviewing the achievements you wrote down and choose the one that appears to you to be the most important. This decision is best made by including your feelings as well as your thoughts. Mark this achievement number one. Then decide which are second, third, fourth, and fifth in order of importance, from your point of view. Mark them two through five. Now number the remaining achievements in any convenient order. You will notice that this entire process is designed to give you increasing insight into the conditions and situations underlying your past achievements. A large part of your job and career success comes from developing the ability to recognize instantly when a given set of circumstances will allow you to be successful and when it won't.

Study the achievement you marked number one and, on a separate page, write down all the Success Factors you can think of relating to this achievement.

When you have finished analyzing your first achievement, put it aside and start a new, complete list of Success Factors pertaining to your second achievement. Soon you will notice that many Success Factors appear over and over in different achievements. Your "success pattern" will begin to emerge. It is as unique as your fingerprint.

Step Three. Combine all the separate listings of Success Factors into one master list on a separate sheet of paper. Write down each Success Factor only once. The order in which you list them is not important.

A partial master list using the above examples of achievements would look like this:

Supervising
Communicating
Liaison
Planning
Organizing
Coordinating
Analysis
Decision Making
Cost Control
Persuading
Delegating
Cooperating
Problem Solving
Human Relations
Art/Design

Step Four. Arrange your Success Factors into groups, in order to understand their meaning in terms of a job and career objective.

Use a new sheet of paper and transfer the first Success Factor, whatever it happens to be, from your master list to this sheet.

Then write under it or next to it any of the other Success Factors from your master list that you feel *directly* relate to it. Using the above example, "Supervising" would be the first Success Factor to be transferred to your new sheet. Two Success Factors you would write down under it would be "decision making" and "delegating." This is your first *Success Factor Group*.

Now pick any of the Success Factors you have not used to form the first group and start a new, separate group. Follow the same procedure as above. Whenever you are in doubt about whether or not a Success Factor relates to one of the groups on this sheet, use it to start a new group. When you are totally unable to decide in which group a Success Factor belongs, include it in more than one group.

This process calls for some arbitrary decisions. Very often your decision to include a Success Factor in one group or another depends on how you feel about the factor, and how you use it in the context of your life: Again, any inappropriate decisions on your part will be corrected later through a special process of testing it against reality.

Continue until all Success Factors have been transferred to the new page and have been assigned to groups. Make sure you cross out Success Factors on your master list as you transfer them to the new sheet.

Typically you end up with six to ten groups. A group can contain any number of Success Factors; it is possible for a group to contain only one Success Factor. Here is an abbreviated example of this step:

MASTER LIST
(Random listing of Success Factors)

Creating
Financial Control
Selling
Showmanship
Problem Solving
Ingenuity
Decision Making
Management
Promoting
Package Design

SUCCESS FACTOR GROUPS

{ Creating
  Package Design
  Ingenuity

{ Showmanship
  Selling
  Promoting

{ Problem Solving
  Ingenuity

{ Financial Control

{ Decision Making
  Management
  Financial Control

Note that "Financial Control" is listed both in the group denoting management and as a separate "group." "Ingenuity" is shown as part of two different groups. In fact, a review of the achievements that produced these Success Factors will tell you to which group or groups they belong, by showing the context from which they originate. For instance, if Financial Control refers to a management achievement, it belongs in the last group. If it originates from an achievement that has nothing to do with management or decision making, it belongs in a separate group.

Step Five. The purpose of this step is to assign a *Key Success Factor* to each of the groups compiled in the previous step. A Key Success Factor is a word or combination of words that represents the most important element of a Success Factor Group. It can be one of the words already contained in the group or an entirely new word not used before.

This step requires a good deal of thought, because Key Success Factors are the bridge between your past and your future. Looking at the first group in the example given above, and depending on the general background of the person involved, the Key Success Factor might be "Sales Promotion." Or it might be "Public Relations."

At this point you may find that a group is too diversified to be summarized in one or two words. You will have to divide it into two groups with different Key Success Factors.

Or you may now wish to combine two groups into one. In the above example, the first and third group could be combined into one, with the Key Success Factor of "Creative Problem Solving."

The Key Success Factors, after thorough "reality testing," will be the main components of your work throughout your career and will be part of any job objective you ever formulate.

Step Six. At this point you will need to make some decision about preference and relative importance.

Which of the Key Success Factors would you most like to use as your main job and career component? Which should be second, third, etc.? You may find that one or two of the Key Factors appear to be of minor importance in your future career and should be eliminated.

Sometimes it is helpful to review the order of Key Success Factors after a day has passed.

To refer again to our example, there is a basic difference between a career built around Sales Promotion and one with Financial Control as its main focus.

You will begin to make some basic career decisions during this step. However, you will have ample opportunity to make adjustments and changes based on additional information and insight.

Step Seven. The information you have developed now has to be tested against "reality."

You have developed a set of success-based elements on which your future career will be built. Are these elements realistic, not only in terms of your own experience, but also in terms of the world of work? Here are three reality tests you can apply singly or in combination that will give you confidence that your work (up to this point) has been valid.

First, write each of your Key Success Factors on a separate sheet of paper and then give as many concrete past accomplishments as you can to prove that you have successfully carried out the kind of activity described by the Key Success Factor.

If one of your Key Success Factors is Creative Problem Solving, try to think of specific experiences where you used your imagination to solve a problem. Some will be contained in your original set of achievements, but you will probably be able to think of additional ones. Make sure that your examples are specific and can have meaning to future employers, although they need not all be achievements that happened during paid employment.

Knowledge of your Key Success Factors and proof that they are "real" will give you an increased feeling of confidence. Now you know who you are and in what direction you are going. No one will be able to stop you.

Second, ask your spouse or a close friend to write down the answers to the following questions: (a) What does he or she consider to be your greatest strengths, talents, and abilities; (b) In what areas do you need to improve; and (c) What conditions and duties do you need in your work in order to be happy?

Ask this person to be as honest and straightforward as possible.

You may object that such information is subjective, not objective. However, in your job and career building, there is no such thing as cold, scientific, objective reality. You can approach it only by getting as many points of reference as possible.

Third, psychological and aptitude tests play a limited value in reality testing. However, they can serve as additional points of reference once original information has been developed through Success Factor Analysis. Any information that corroborates your conclusions will increase your self-confidence. Information that appears to contradict any part of your Success Factor Analysis will serve as a red flag. Contradictory information makes it necessary to ask more questions and resolve the apparent discrepancy. But you will always find the answer in Success Factor Analysis, based on your achievements.

Vocational interest inventories (which, strictly speaking, are not tests at all) can serve the same useful purpose. They are available through many educational institutions. When taking such an inventory, it is well to remember that it cannot tell you what you should do. A high score as a psychologist, for example, does not tell you that you should become a psychologist. It simply means that you have certain interests in common with the group of psychologists who were used as a standard when the interest inventory was developed.

The value of tests and interest inventories depends on how they are used and who interprets them. They can add very little information to Success Factor Analysis, but in the hands of an experienced career counselor, they can reinforce the information you have gained.

Step Eight. You are now ready to write the first draft of a *functional job objective*. The word "functional" refers to the functions, activities, or duties you would like to be part of a job. Because these functions are identical with your Key Success Factors, which in turn are derived from your achievements, they will ensure job and career satisfaction as well as success.

The best way to avoid a traumatic experience at this point is to write a tentative functional job objective in an informal way. Remember, you are talking only about *what* you want to do; it's too soon to say *where* you want to do it. You are also not concerned with job titles at this point. Here is an excellent way to start: "I would like a job where I can use my ability to . . . which will result in . . ."

For example: "I would like a job where my experience in sales promotion, supported by creative problem solving and cost control abilities, will result in profitable decisions and sales increases."

When creating a functional job objective, it is important to develop early habits of thinking—not only of "what do I want?" but "what will I contribute?" Be aware of this mutuality not only in work relationships but in all human relationships. It is the lubricant that makes lives and careers go at a smoother pace.

At this stage, you don't need to be concerned about writing a formal statement for use on your resume. But you must feel that any job that fits your description would be ideal for you. Feel free to rewrite this informal objective until it sounds good to you.

Be sure to make clear which of the job functions you wish to focus on. In the sample objective given above, the focus is on Sales Promotion. If Cost Control responsibility is your center of interest, you would have to rewrite the functional job objective accordingly.

Step Nine. Although you are not ready to go out into the job market, your job and career objective is incomplete without some reference to a possible job environment. You know what you want to do, but you may be unsure of where you are going to do it.

Whatever your job and career objective, whatever your experience and occupational level, whatever your age, the incredible richness and variety of the job market is more than one source of information can reveal. I am not talking about openings; you'll learn how to find those in the coming chapters. I am referring to the variety of professional and occupational settings and opportunities.

To begin your preliminary market research, take stock of what you already know: Your current knowledge includes job environments you have experienced in your working life up to this point. It may include environments you know through friends and relatives. It may also include work environments you have experienced through your avocations, or as a customer or client. For instance, if your avocation is restoring antique furniture, you probably have a working knowledge of the antique business.

Your aim at this point is to expand your range of possibilities, not to make career decisions based on your current knowledge of possible job environments.

There is only one way to evaluate job environments. Will they allow you to use your greatest strengths and skills, your Key Success Factors? Will they allow you to implement your functional job objective? For instance, using our previous example, your objective of sales promotion could not be implemented in an organization that sells nothing. But this still leaves a multitude of possible job environments.

Even at this early stage, you can make some decisions: outdoor vs. indoor; product vs. service; profit vs. nonprofit. You can explore possible geographic, architectural, and human environments. But guard against writing off entire sectors of the work world based on prejudgment and lack of firsthand information.

You may have made a decision already. You may feel that, at this time in your life, a career change would be too risky. But consider the great variety of possibilities even within one profession. Any lawyer, computer analyst, artist, or teacher has multiple choices available.

The information is all around you. Your library is full of printed materials on every conceivable occupational field. You will quickly develop your own personal radar and will see and hear ideas everywhere. Even television commercials can serve this purpose.

Start a list of occupational environments that capture your interest. Write down names of companies and other organizations that appeal to you. Evaluate all ideas by checking them against your functional job objective. Talk with friends and acquaintances. Most good information comes through word of mouth.

When you have at least a dozen possibilities written down on your list, check for common denominators. If you find that all the choices tend toward technical/scientific job environments, you can include that in your functional job objective. If you find an affinity for publishing, social service, or consumer goods, incorporate that into your objective.

You may not be able to make a decision based on the information on your list. It is perfectly reasonable to enter the job market to explore a number of different environments, as long as you have a clearly stated purpose. You know what you want to do, even though you may not have decided on the ideal environment in which to do it.

Many doors are opened to a person with a clear purpose. And through Success Factor Analysis, you have identified and clarified that purpose.

The following is a summary of the objective-setting process:

1. Write down ten to fifteen achievements.
2. Identify your Success Factors.
3. Compile a master list of Success Factors.
4. Arrange Success Factors into groups.

5. Identify and assign a Key Success Factor to each group.
6. Rank Key Success Factors in order of importance to you.
7. "Reality-test" each Key Success Factor.
8. Write your functional job objective

You now have a job objective. It should reflect all the elements of your long-term career plan.

Before we go on to the next chapter. "The Job and Career Market," I would like to say a few words about adverse career factors that affect career planning and objective setting. Your objective, for instance, may be imaginative but, for a number of reasons, may not be achievable in the real world. This can happen in several ways: You may not be physically or legally qualified for certain professions. For example, a client of ours, who was a professional pilot, became so nearsighted that he had to give up flying. By recognizing and using his Key Success Factors, he implemented a career in facilities management. He is now the manager of a small airport in the western United States.

Your objective may not be achievable because you are not sufficiently trained or experienced for a position at the responsibility level you want. By entering professions at a lower level, and making a detailed plan to gain the knowledge and experience needed, you can overcome this problem.

However, do not aimlessly sign up for courses and accumulate degrees, because that can seriously delay and sidetrack your career. Acquire knowledge that reinforces your strengths. Don't spend mental and physical energy on becoming more proficient in an area of weakness and low motivation.

Your Success Factors are a reliable guide that tells you where to apply the energy for growth. For most people, adverse career factors and weaknesses are cancelled out by the knowledge and positive use of Success Factors and career strengths.

You will never have to say that your career isn't moving ahead and that you don't like your work if you develop the habit of repeating your Success Factor Analysis once a year. You will have new achievements each year. By analyzing them as described in this chapter, you will add new self-knowledge and speed up career advancement.

5
The
Job and Career
Market

Revolutionize your view of the job market by discarding the myth that your only chance for finding a job is as a result of a job opening or vacancy. *Every time someone is doing a job, there is a potential job opening.* In addition, new jobs are created every day in most occupational fields, some of them based on entirely new concepts. The job market is far richer and more varied than you may realize.

The job market is also the career market, because careers are made up of individual jobs. To find these jobs and build careers, you need an accurate picture of the job market and how it works.

This chapter shows you how to find accurate job market information and how to use it in the context of your job and career objectives.

How do jobs become available to you? Certainly there is a job opportunity every time there is a job vacancy. There is also a job opportunity every time there is a *potential* vacancy—when someone is about to leave a job or to be terminated. But very few people know about it.

There is a job opportunity every time an organization has a

need that is not being met or a problem that is not being solved. There are multiple job opportunities when an organization is expanding. There are even job opportunities when an organization is contracting: People are needed who can (1) wear more than one hat, (2) replace unproductive employees, and (3) help make an unprofitable business profitable.

General employment figures and statistics are rarely helpful in understanding the job market as it relates to your own job and career objectives. Statistics can even lead to unjustified negative assumptions and defeat. A negative interpretation of high unemployment statistics may discourage you. Worse, it may lead you to accept a bad job situation and prolonged suffering, when closer investigation might have shown that the bulk of the unemployment figures come from a part of the job market not related to your objectives.

A positive and correct view of the job market allows you to see 10 percent unemployment in terms of 90 percent employment. These are excellent odds for someone with a purpose and the will to achieve it. This juxtaposition also demolishes the myth that the negative interpretation of information is the more realistic one, and that optimism leads to unrealistic idealism.

There is a direct relationship in job and career building between expectations and results. The highest expectations lead to the greatest results.

High expectations are perfectly compatible with realistic expectations, if you have accurate information on which to base them. How do you get this information? Every *unsuccessful* job seeker will shower you with tons of misinformation, proving beyond the shadow of a doubt that there are no current job opportunities worth having in your field and that the outlook is bleak for years to come. Successful people are too busy working at their jobs to volunteer a lot of information. Yet they are the primary sources of reliable facts. Chap-

ter 6 describes a step-by-step method for making contact with
successful people.

The value of getting accurate inside information is illustrated by the experience of a senior-level client. A man in his forties, he wanted to combine his engineering skill with his love
for stereo equipment. He was planning a career change from
vibration control engineering to the manufacturing of audio
equipment.

He visited some of the major firms in his chosen field. The
information he received amounted to a picture of gloom and
disaster. At that time the entire industry was in the doldrums.
But of eight senior executives he talked with, five mentioned
in passing that there was one small company that appeared to
buck the general trend in the industry and had, in fact, grown
considerably during the past year.

Our client wrote to the chairman of the board of that small
company and described the compliments paid to the firm by
five well-known people in the field. The client got a first interview, several follow-up interviews, and finally the offer of
an executive position. He has since been instrumental in helping the company continue its spectacular growth. His success
in getting the job was due to his ability to isolate useful information from the mass of negative and depressing statistics.

A second way to obtain accurate information on employment trends and conditions relevant to your particular career
field is the study of professional and trade publications. Almost every occupational field generates its own journals, periodicals, newsletters, or other printed information. Some of
these are generally available, some through subscription only,
and many can be found at libraries.

An excellent source of information regarding publications
which contain names of key people in a vast number of occupational categories is *Bernard Klein's Guide to American Directories*, published by Bernard Klein Publications, Inc., Rye,

New York. Many of the directories and brochures listed are low in cost. The more expensive ones are available at libraries.

Visit your local public library. Familiarity with its personnel and the research material available in your chosen career field as well as related fields is one of your greatest resources. It is second only to personal contact with people in your field, which must always be your primary source of information.

An auxiliary information resource on the job market, if your job and career objectives are in the business world, is to read *The Wall Street Journal* and *Business Week* regularly. But take care to consider the sources given for all information and accept *nothing* as factual until you have had an opportunity to check it with a living, breathing person who is qualified to corroborate its accuracy and value. This can sometimes alert you to trends and opportunities that you might otherwise have overlooked.

A so-called job cooperative, a self-help group of job seekers, can be a source of good information and mutual confidence building *if* it is guided by an experienced and knowledgeable person. Without such guidance, a job cooperative can turn into a source of misery and misinformation.

There is one set of job market statistics that is relevant to all job seekers, regardless of their particular job and career objectives. It is the statistical breakdown of how people actually find jobs. The following figures were taken from Haldane client files:

70% to 75% of all jobs are never advertised. Information about these jobs never reaches the media or the job brokers but is passed from person to person by word of mouth. This is called the "informal job market."

10% to 20% of all jobs are obtained through printed advertisements in newspapers, periodicals, or other publications. There are also a number of organizations who, for a fee, supply compilations or digests of such published job market information.

5% to 10% of all jobs are obtained through job brokers, such as employment agencies, recruiters and search firms. If your salary expectation is low, and you are in a field in which jobs are plentiful, you have a better chance of finding a job through an agency. However, the placement rate of every type of employment agency decreases with increasing responsibility and salary levels, and the number of senior executives who obtained their current positions through a job broker is minimal. The last two categories together are called the "formal job market."

2% to 4% of all jobs are obtained through sources not included in the other categories, such as some union hiring, civil service listings, or in-company listings of job openings.

These figures are facts of life and have been virtually unchanged for decades. They apply to men and women, and to blue-collar as well as white-collar workers. They have been continuously supported by all known studies published by government and independent organizations. (See chart.)

These statistics describe not only how people get jobs, but how jobs get people. Most of the important positions in any organization are filled without recourse to advertising or job brokers. In some cases, publication of job opportunities is a legal requirement, but studies have shown that many of those published positions are, in fact, filled through informal means.

An understanding of how the job market works will save you weeks and even months in your search. An efficient and productive job search consists of a combination of *all* available approaches, but in the right proportion, according to the expected results documented above.

In any discussion of job market strategy, the first step is to get information about the job market that is relevant to your job and career objectives. The second step is to act on that information and to convert it into tangible opportunities.

If your information sources tell you that the job market in your career field is tight, that the field is overcrowded or is in

How People Get Jobs

U.S. Dept. of Labor

Blue-collar and White-collar

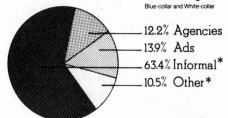

12.2% Agencies

13.9% Ads

63.4% Informal*

10.5% Other*

The U.S. government conducted a comprehensive survey in 1973 to determine how American workers find jobs.

The study included all categories of wage and salary workers, except farm workers – from professionals and administrators, to construction workers and mechanics.

The sample consisted of 10.4 million men and women who had found new jobs, and the chart shows the methods by which their jobs had been obtained.

(*Jobseeking Methods Used by American Workers*, U.S. Department of Labor, Bureau of Labor Statistics, Bulletin #1886. 1975.)

Granovetter (Harvard)

Professional-Technical-Managerial

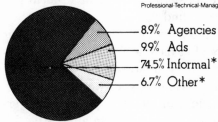

8.9% Agencies

9.9% Ads

74.5% Informal*

6.7% Other*

Mark S. Granovetter, a sociologist at Harvard University, investigated how people get jobs. His study included professional, technical, and managerial workers who had recently found jobs, and the chart shows the methods by which their jobs had been obtained.

Granovetter's data also indicate that of the people who found jobs through personal contacts, 43.8% had new positions created for them.

Granovetter concludes: "Personal contacts are of paramount importance in connecting people with jobs. Better jobs are found through contacts, and the best jobs, the ones with the highest pay and prestige and affording the greatest satisfaction to those in them, are most apt to be filled in this way."

(Granovetter, *Getting a Job: A Study of Contacts and Careers*. Harvard University Press, Cambridge, 1974.)

Bernard Haldane Associates

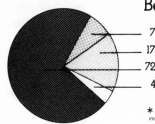

7% Agencies

17% Ads

72% Informal*

4% Other*

This diagram shows how 4,800 Haldane clients got jobs in a recent 12-month period.

* Informal methods of job finding are those whereby the job seekers exercise their own initiative in building on personal contacts and making themselves known to potential employers. They are differentiated from formal methods, which rely on advertisements and/or employment agencies.

Other is a residual category, which encompasses such methods of job finding as trade union hiring and civil service.

fact "closed," you will have to make some decisions. Begin by checking the reliability of your sources and the accuracy of your information. Develop further contacts and resources. Remember, only information from people *productively active* in your chosen field is of value. Secondhand information from outsiders looking in, or unsuccessful insiders, is worth very little.

Determine your odds: What is the number of jobs in your career area? What is the turnover rate? What are your emotional and financial resources, in case of a prolonged job search?

You have several choices.

You may decide to settle for nothing less than an ideal job, no matter how long it takes to find it.

Or you may allocate a finite length of time to conduct your search for the ideal position, but have a "Plan B" in readiness if you don't succeed in the time you have given yourself.

A Plan B is formulated by reviewing your Key Success Factors and recombining them in a different way, with a different emphasis. This will allow you to choose an alternative job objective while still using all your skills, talents, and experience.

Another approach available to you is the indirect one, where you target for a position different from, but related to, your chosen job objective. From there you can plan to move to your ideal job in one or more steps.

What you can never afford to do is to give up your career objective and settle for a noncareer job together with a meaningless life.

The following examples will illustrate different, but valid, solutions to the same problem.

Two of our clients obtained PhDs in relatively limited fields from a major university during the same year. Both knew that entry into a teaching position would require patience, persistence, and financial resources, because there were fewer than twenty positions in each of their fields nationwide, and the rate of turnover was very low.

The first client made a decision to hold out for one of the scarce professorships. In reviewing his assets, he recognized that patience and perseverance were among his strongest Success Factors. By a combination of part-time positions and family support, he was able to survive financially. During the next two years, he used all his free time to establish himself in his chosen field. He realized he would have to be known to authorities in this field as a man of superior capability and knowledge. He worked hard and long hours and corresponded frequently with the people who held important positions in his career area. When the time came, he was their natural choice for the opening. Because he had estimated that it might take him five years to achieve his goals, he was elated when success came in less than half that time.

The second client solved his problem in a different way. He reviewed his Key Success Factors and examined them in the light of strong interest and motivation. He found that his ability and liking for financial decision-making was high on the list and would have been used to a very limited extent in a teaching job. So, he revised his job objective and, after an intensive job search of several months, joined a government agency. His job consisted of making judgments about research grants and endowments given to academic institutions doing work in his field.

A good example of the Plan B approach is a woman client whose job objective was to become a freelance writer on technical subjects. After a few weeks of researching her market, she found out from other self-employed writers that a considerable amount of time and effort had to be spent on self-marketing in order to get a start in that profession. It would take time to build an adequate income. She decided on a two-step approach to becoming a self-employed technical writer. First, she joined the publications department of a major technical company. The quality of the company's brochures, manuals, and sales literature helped her establish her reputation in the field, and her contacts with designers, graphic artists, and printers proved valuable. When she became self-employed a year later, she found it much easier to generate business and income than many freelance writers who had been working in the field for years.

To summarize: Accurate and up-to-date job market information, and the correct use of that information, leads to career control. If you are in control of your own career, you are in control of a large part of your life.

6
Contacts

A good job and a good career depend on good information. As you have seen in the last chapter, this information is available in many ways, such as help wanted advertisements, employment agencies, and other sources. But the most important information, leading to the best jobs and the most fulfilling careers, comes through word of mouth, through contacts. Contacts lead to interviews, interviews lead to jobs, and jobs lead to careers.

In this chapter you will learn how to get this important information. You will learn how to identify and make contact with those people who have the best information. Let's start by defining the term *contact*.

A contact is, first, a person with whom you establish a mutually beneficial relationship. This is a very different view from the commonly held assumption that a contact is a person who can pull strings for you, who can give you a job or find one for you. Contacts must be seen as sources of information. They will help you make informed decisions about your career, and you will share your own information with them.

Every contact you make is in touch with other people who have important information, people you should meet and know. So a contact is, second, a source of referrals, a route of access to other people and other information that, directly or indirectly, leads to job and career opportunities.

A contact can, in some cases, be the person who offers you a job. But the main purpose of a contact is to establish a productive relationship in which valuable, mutually beneficial information is exchanged.

Using contacts to ask for a job is like asking for a handout. It places that contact in the embarrassing position of being asked for something he or she may not have. On the other hand, asking for information and advice is an acknowledgment that the person is important enough to have valuable information. It is a request for something that people are usually willing to give.

Which contacts are valuable and which are not?

People who do what *you* would like to do, and do it well, are among the most important contacts you can have. The leaders in your profession, or in the profession you would like to get into, are the ideal contacts. Successful people in any profession are important contacts, because they tend to understand the process of achieving success and can help others to understand it. The same is true of people who enjoy what they do. For very practical reasons, people who deal with other people and know large numbers of them are useful contacts, too. And actively retired persons can often be among the most valuable contacts you can find, for they can provide a wealth of insight into the work world in general, and their former professions in particular.

Throughout your career you need to be constantly in touch with who is doing what in your profession. Experience shows that to be in the right place at the right time is the most effective way to advance your career. The best way to accomplish this is to be in many places at all times. You need to be in touch with the people who make things happen, or have made things happen, in your field or in related fields.

How do you know who these people are, and how do you get to them?

Fortunately, thousands of successful job and career builders have shown that it takes only three or four steps to get to talk to anyone in this country, no matter how important his or her position. The connecting links to the President of the United States, for instance, might consist of your local congressmen, senators and their staffs, cabinet officers, and members of the President's staff.

While most people will accept that there are routes of access even to presidents, job seekers often think that successful access requires an "aggressive" person. You may assume that the success of making contacts depends on an aggressive approach, because you may have been told that, to get a job, you must sell yourself.

The fact is that an aggressive attitude usually gets in the way. It is true that there is a time and a place for selling yourself. But in making contacts and in creating a contact network, you are in the process of establishing productive human relationships. These relationships always are better accomplished by being "purposeful" rather than by being "aggressive."

Another attitude that interferes with making successful contacts is expressed by the words "Why should anyone want to see me?" You will learn that, as well as receiving information, you will be in a position to give important information, information that your contact wants and needs. *In order to get, you must give.* This give and take, above all, makes the process of making contacts work.

The building of a contact network is a first prerequisite. "But," you may say, "I don't have any contacts to start with."

The answer is that all of us have access to people. Once you understand that a contact is someone with whom you establish a relationship to exchange information, you are ready to identify a variety of people you know, who are the contacts you will start with. (The popular view of contacts as "people who can get you a job" falls apart very quickly during a period of adversity.)

You may already be a member of what is called an old boy network. This term is most often associated with the academic world. The people with whom you went to school are members of such a network. But, in a larger sense, this term applies to any group formed by a common experience, or even sometimes by being members of the same social class.

Being a member of such an old boy network can be beneficial and can serve as a starting point for a personal contact network of your own. But experience shows that most people misuse this type of contact.

A young man who graduated with honors from a major university was looking for a job. He wrote letters and made telephone calls to many of his fellow graduates and some of his professors. They were all glad to refer him to others. After thirty-eight interviews he started to be referred to the same people for the second or third time. He was no further ahead than he had been at the beginning, because he was being referred only to members of his old boy network. He had asked thirty-eight people if they knew of a job opening. When asked what kind of job he was looking for, he said he didn't know, but he'd recognize the right job when it came along. If a job search is to be effective, a career direction or purpose is essential. Only when the job seeker has defined his purpose can he distinguish between leads that may be helpful and leads that will only move him in circles.

Some prospective Haldane clients say: "I never needed help in finding a job; I have always found jobs on my own." Whatever the merits of these statements, one thing we know is that no one gets a job without the help of at least one other person, the employer, and usually one or more persons who provided the information which led to the job. However, there is one element of truth in these words: To the extent that you must take the initiative in finding a job and building a career, you can be said to be on your own.

The first step is to identify the bridges to your future contact network. The bridges are provided by people you already know but may never have thought of as contacts. They are people with whom you feel comfortable and with whom you can talk easily.

Write down the names of several people you know from the following categories: anyone who provides a service and deals with people constantly, such as lawyers, doctors, dentists, accountants, civic and community leaders, politicians, clergymen; anyone who earns his or her living by making contacts, such as salespeople, insurance, real estate and stockbrokers, public relations and advertising specialists; anyone important in the business community, such as business owners, executives, business consultants, and bankers. Include former employers and business associates, as well as members of your family, friends, and neighbors, whatever their professions are. Members of the academic community, such as professors, deans, and college presidents also can be excellent starting contacts.

Now select three people from this list, using one or more criteria. Besides being easy to talk with, the contacts should have life experience. Preferably they should be mature individuals who have found reasonable success and fulfillment in what they do and are used to dealing with people through their professional or social activities. These are the *primary contacts*.

It may never be necessary to use more than three of these primary contacts, because the goal is to build a network of *new* contacts. The purpose of working with primary contacts is to get used to the water, to get initial reaction to your market campaign preparation, and to build a bridge between that preparation and making contacts with strangers.

At this stage of contact building, you need to know if there are any flaws in your presentation. People with whom you already have a good relationship respond more openly to a request for criticism than do those you are meeting for the first time. If your resume looks impressive only to you, you must know about it now and improve it. If you talk about your job objective and your abilities unconvincingly, you must learn that now and correct it.

By giving you a frank and open critique of how you come across, your primary contacts will become involved in your job and career campaign. As a result, primary contacts are likely to share information you never realized they had. One of the greatest exercises in futility is the job seeker who decides, "Oh, I already know what he's going to say!" This statement is a common block to the flow of information.

Interviews with primary contacts *always* result in an improvement in the job seeker's presentation. These interviews frequently produce some information of value about the job market, and they almost always generate one or more referrals.

The method of planning and carrying out what we call a Referral interview is described below. The Referral interview is essentially the same both for people you already know and people you have not met before. Note that unless an interviewer identifies a specific job opportunity that he is considering you for, you are not on a job interview, you are on a Referral interview. If a job is discussed, it is a job interview. *All* other interviews are Referral interviews.

There are five purposes to accomplish in each Referral interview. During the beginning stages of a Referral campaign, the emphasis will be mainly on sharpening your presentation, developing your ability to ask questions, to get information, and to feel at ease with the process. During the latter stages, you will increasingly be speaking with people in your own field, and the emphasis will be on eliciting specific job market information.

The description of the Referral interview will be given first, followed by the method for setting up such interviews. The chronological sequence is purposely reversed. Once you have become familiar with the Referral concept, it will be easy to understand and implement the simple steps required to set up these interviews.

The first and most important purpose of a Referral interview is to *establish rapport* with the interviewer. Without involvement on the personal level on the part of the interviewer, nothing else happens.

How do you establish this rapport?

It is easier for you if you are talking with a primary contact. But in all cases, the interviewer must have a clear understanding of what your job and career objective is. You, in turn, must take a genuine interest in your interviewer. Most of your interviewers are in the process of career growth and development themselves. They will appreciate and repay the interest you show in them. Listen to what they say and show your appreciation by responding positively.

Frequently the environment in which you meet an interviewer tells a lot about him or her. For example, during a Referral interview with a senior insurance executive, a Haldane client noticed that all the pictures on the wall of the executive's office had a common theme: airplanes. The client commented on this, and it developed that the insurance executive was a former flight instructor who had changed careers successfully ten years ago. Because the subject of mid-life career change was one of the client's major interests, the ensuing conversation formed a bond between the two men which helped them build rapport.

One of the questions frequently asked about Referral interviews is this: "Should I do advance research on my prospective interviewer and on his company?"

The time to find out about the interviewer is during the interview, and the person to get the information from is the interviewer. This is not only an excellent rapport-building tool, provided you ask with genuine interest, but gets much better information.

In the process of a Referral campaign, you will learn to sharpen your observation through constant practice and improve your ability to establish rapport. Some of the great men and women in the world are known to have the ability to establish this rapport instantly, to shut out all but their concern for the other person at the first contact.

Your expectations in an interview with a contact will *always* be met. If you are purposeful, if you expect to give as well as get information, this expectation will be communicated to your contact. Thousands of job seekers have told us that they usually got the results they expected, good or bad, in interviews with contacts. Your attitude will determine the interviewer's attitude. If you expect an interviewer to share his or her knowledge and thoughts freely, you will receive that benefit. If, on the other hand, you anticipate lack of interest by the interviewer, that expectation will be met, too.

It is up to you, during the beginning stages of the interview, to explain your purpose in such a way that the interviewer understands it and wants to help. The words you use might go something like this: "I'm in the process of taking the next step in my career. I want to make sure I'm doing this right. Mr./ Mrs. X (the person who referred you) told me about you and suggested you might be able to answer some important questions for me. Neither Mr./Mrs. X nor I expect you to know of a job opening, but the information you can give me would be very valuable and would help me plan my next step." Then describe your job and career objective and some of the steps you have taken up to this point in your market campaigns.

The second purpose of a Referral interview is to obtain the interviewer's *reaction* to how you present your job and career objective, both in conversation and in written form, through your resume and other supporting material. Do you make sense? Do you come across believably? Can you back up your job objective with skills, interest, and accomplishments that show it to be realistic?

This is the moment of truth. You must be sincere in asking for this feedback, and you must be willing to listen to it. Because most of your interviewers have gone through job and career changes themselves, their advice is worth getting. You may not always find it compatible with your personality and expectations, but you should always appreciate and acknowledge it.

By taking an interest in your past, present, and future, the interviewer will get involved in what you are doing and share in your excitement. He or she will want to help you open new possibilities and opportunities and, in a real sense, become an ally.

The third purpose of a Referral interview is to obtain hard *information*. All of us know certain facts about the job market in general and certain facets of it in particular. But each of us has only one segment of the total range of knowledge available. The more segments you can add to your own, the more knowledge you have, and the more easily you can navigate in the job market.

Each of your interviewers has knowledge from which you can benefit, but it is not always easy to elicit that knowledge. Be prepared to ask questions.

Many opportunities for asking questions become evident during the interview. So sharpen your ability to seize opportunities as they appear. One Haldane client in the computer field reported that he spoke with a lawyer with whom he had been acquainted for some years. During the interview the lawyer mentioned in an offhand manner that he had had lunch on the previous day with the president of a major computer firm. Our client picked up the thread at this point and expressed his interest. He got not only information about the firm's recent success in introducing a new minicomputer, but also a personal referral to the president.

During the first interviews with your primary contacts, you will, of course, not ask specific questions that require a knowledge outside the interviewer's profession. But whenever you are talking with a person in your profession, or a related one, here are a few types of questions you might ask: "Who is doing what in my field? Which organizations in my profession are doing well and which aren't? What professional periodicals or trade magazines are the best to subscribe to or read (when entering a new career area)?" And even, "What income level can I expect to reach with my background and qualifications?"

This last question illustrates that there is hardly any subject you can't raise during a Referral interview. However, ask only questions to which you genuinely need answers. Requests for information should never be a routine or gimmick. They would only destroy the rapport that has been established. In fact, you are hardly likely to run out of valid questions. No matter what professional level you are on, the more you know, the more you become aware of what you don't know.

However much you are aware of the importance of obtaining information during an interview, few job seekers realize that they actually possess a wealth of information that can, in turn, benefit the interviewer. The job seeker's existence and future availability, in itself, is valuable information to the interviewer. Here again, mutuality of interest is important.

A client who had developed great skill in the marketing

field, but became increasingly bored with the product he had been involved with, thought that the application of comprehensive marketing techniques to banking was an idea whose time had come. He started a Referral campaign. After four productive interviews with senior banking executives, he found that he knew more about the possibilities of bank marketing than most of the people he met. He simply put together his marketing knowledge with the information about development problems in banking he obtained through asking questions on his Referral interviews. He became a very sought-after person and is now pursuing a brilliant career in this field.

This aspect of the Referral interview is especially important to the person at the beginning of his or her career. It presents a golden opportunity for getting information that may never again present itself.

People who have advanced in their careers remember how they started. They remember the help they received and the help they wished they had received. If approached in the right way, all of us are inclined to share our knowledge of the work world with those who are engaged in a job or career change.

This aspect of the Referral interview is a boon especially to the woman who is entering the job market either for the first time or after a prolonged absence. Here is an opportunity to become knowledgeable about the current attitudes she is likely to encounter, prejudices she may have to deal with, business terminology she may need to learn, and areas of opportunity newly opened to women.

One question *never* to ask during a Referral interview is "Do you have a job for me?" Whatever form this question takes, whether it is "Do you know someone who can use my services?" or "Can you refer me to someone who can use my abilities or background?" it is taboo because the implied contract of the Referral interview—"I don't expect you to know of a job"—is broken. A request for a job or a job lead would be an embarrassment to the interviewer. No one likes to say no, and we all tend to resent being asked for a favor we are not in a position to grant.

Another question *never* to ask any interviewer is "What kind of job should I be looking for?" This is like asking "What should I do with my life?" No reasonable person feels qualified to answer such questions. Before beginning a Referral campaign, have a clear idea of the direction in which you want your career to go. What you need is information on how to locate the best possible opportunity for the Next Step in that career.

In addition to your resume, what further tools do you need on a Referral interview? You should bring a small notebook with you but only to record specific information, such as names of organizations and people. Many interviewers are irritated by someone taking notes constantly. It gives them the feeling they are talking into a tape recorder. It can also seriously interfere with your ability to listen and respond to what the interviewer is saying.

A Referral interview should take twenty to thirty minutes. Some of the best and most successful interviews in the experience of Bernard Haldane Associates' clients have taken less than fifteen minutes. During the first few moments, promise the busy interviewer that you'll be brief. By keeping the interview short, you demonstrate that you know the value of your interviewer's and your own time.

The fourth purpose of a Referral interview is to *continue building a contact network* by asking for one or more referrals. The person you are talking with is now part of your personal contact network. He or she is also, knowingly or unknowingly, part of many other contact networks.

Referrals should be asked for at the end of an interview,

and only when you are sure you have succeeded in establishing rapport with the interviewer, as shown by the fact that he or she has given good advice and information. Again, remember that all of us achieve goals with the help of others. Every mature interviewer knows this. The fact that he or she has agreed to see you, and is talking with you, is evidence of that.

Be ready to explain your purpose in asking for a referral. This requires practice. What you say must be reasonable in the context of each interview. This might be a good approach: "You have been very helpful! I appreciate the information you have given me. I now would like to talk to a few people about (areas which are outside this interviewer's knowledge)" or ". . . people who are in (leading positions in your field of interest). Can you suggest one or two people in this area, or someone who knows such a person?" It should be made clear to the interviewer, in any case, that you have no intention of asking his or her referrals for a job.

Some interviewers may need to give some time and thought to your request for referrals. Offer them a few days to think about exactly with whom they would advise you to talk. The conversation may go something like this:

If an interviewer says, for instance, "I can't think of anyone right now," you can assume that he means exactly what he says. You should then respond by saying something like: "I realize you may not have been prepared for such a request. Would it be all right if I called you next Wednesday? You may be able to think of someone by then." Sometimes interviewers show that they have misunderstood your request by what they say. If the response to your request for referrals is "I don't know of anyone who can give you a job," you have an opportunity to correct the impression that you were asking for a job lead.

Remember: You are looking for quality in referrals, not quantity; one good referral is better than ten mediocre ones.

Often you will receive superior referrals by this deferred method, *provided* you set a follow-up date and call the interviewer back on that date.

You will have mastered the art of contact building when you are given contacts during your Referral interviews without asking for them. You will have learned how to communicate your needs and intentions with very few words. The fact that this has happened in thousands of cases over the thirty years of Bernard Haldane Associates' existence shows that the Referral method of contact making is in line with common sense and normal human behavior.

Unless otherwise specified, you may use the interviewer's name when you contact a person to whom he or she referred you. It is also advantageous for you to get as much information as possible from your interviewer about that person. Besides showing that you are genuinely interested in meeting him or her, it strengthens your approach and virtually assures you a good reception.

The fifth and final purpose of a Referral interview is to make sure that the interviewer *remembers you actively*. Ask for permission to keep him or her informed about your progress. This not only will be given, it will be appreciated. Every interviewer, having become part of your contact network, now has a stake in your success. All of us feel good about contributing to someone else's achievement. In the course of time, other thoughts and ideas will come to your interviewers that they will want to share with you, always provided you have left a favorable impression in their minds.

It is, of course, up to you to take the initiative to make the calls and to write the letters necessary to keep your contacts informed. With proper follow-up, you can have your entire contact network actively working in your behalf. You have in effect recruited a sales force!

Now that you have used your interviewers as a resource, it is important to offer to do the same for them, and mean it, should the opportunity arise. You might say something like this: "You've helped me a great deal by what you told me during this interview, and I'm grateful. If there is ever any way I can be of help to you, please let me know." Some interviewers are in doubt that they have been really helpful to you, and it is important for you to tell them, in so many words, that they have helped.

What should your response be when an interviewer, during a bona fide Referral interview, starts talking about a specific job opportunity? Should you ignore or reject it? After all, you told the interviewer you didn't expect to be offered a job or be given a job lead.

Your response should be to reaffirm your original intentions without rejecting the opportunity. You might say something like this: "As you know, I didn't expect you to know of a job opportunity, and it wasn't my purpose to ask you for one, but I'm flattered that you mentioned this to me. Yes, I'd be interested in knowing more about it."

It is usually better to set up another meeting to discuss any specific job opportunity. Then, when you return for the job interview, the interviewer will know why you are there, and you can concentrate on your new purposes for the second meeting.

To summarize, the five purposes of the Referral interview are:

- First, establish rapport with your interviewer.
- Second, get your interviewer's reaction to how you present yourself during the interview, as well as advice on how to improve, expand, and sharpen the presentation of your purposes, your job and career objective, and the data and materials you bring in support of this objective.

- Third, obtain specific up-to-date information about the job market in general and developments in your professional area in particular.
- Fourth, obtain one or two referrals to people who can help you continue the process of building a contact network and who can add to the knowledge you have gained in the previous interviews.
- Fifth, be remembered actively.

How do you go about setting up a Referral interview?

The first step is a letter of approach. This is a warm, personal yet brief letter in which you ask for an interview. It should contain all of the following that are applicable: If the person is a primary contact, why did you choose him or her? If you have been referred to the person, who referred you and why was this person chosen? What is your current employment situation? What is your purpose in asking for an interview? What is your job and career objective?

Also in your letter of approach, make it clear to the recipient that you don't expect him to have or know about a job, and state that you will phone to set up a mutually convenient time for an appointment.

A less formal approach may be used for the interviews with primary contacts. But make sure your primary contacts are aware that this is an important occasion. Often, when in doubt about whether to send a letter asking a primary contact for an interview or just telephoning him or her, write an informal letter. This will underline the fact that you are in the process of making a move of great importance to you.

The second step to setting up a Referral interview is a telephone call. The purposes of the phone call are to follow up the letter and to get a date and time for the appointment. You want to set up the interview, not conduct it over the phone.

The third step is the actual interview, described above.

And the fourth step is a thank-you letter. *Always* write a thank-you letter. It should be warm, sincere, tell specifically how you benefited from the interview, and state that you want to keep the interviewer informed about your progress. The thank-you letter is *the* great way to become actively remembered.

The letter of approach, the telephone call, and a thank-you letter are described in more detail in the following chapter, "Building Communications." It is important to understand, at this point, that each time you skip one of these steps, you reduce the effectiveness of the Referral process by 25 percent. In the experience of thousands of Haldane clients, those who followed each of the four steps got better and faster results than those who took shortcuts.

Each interview and each subsequent contact with that person should be carefully documented. Get into the habit of maintaining a contact diary or folder in which you keep brief, written notes of each interview.

The notes should include the following: the interviewer's name and address; the date and place of the meeting; the interviewer's title, if appropriate; and a brief description of his or her skills and interests, vocational or avocational, for instant recall of the rapport you have established (if an interviewer tells you he rides a bicycle to work each day, for instance, note that for future reference). Also, summarize the interview, describe possible future contact with the interviewer, and note actions that have been planned as a result of the meeting. Copies of all correspondence you have with that person, even brief notes of telephone conversations, should be part of the record.

Sometimes job seekers become aware of an outstanding person in their profession or a leader in their community with whom they would like to make contact. But they may have no referral to that person. Here is one of the clear benefits of record keeping. Often someone in your personal contact network can give you a direct or indirect referral to the person you'd like to meet. By reviewing your records of past interviews, you can usually identify one or more people from whom you can get such a referral.

The Referral approach is also the best method known to neutralize or circumvent prejudice and discrimination in the job market. You will rarely, and never knowingly, be referred to anyone who is likely to discriminate against people like you. And all of us belong to a number of minority groups, whether we have too much or too little formal education, are too old or too young, have had too few or too many jobs, are men or women, etc.

There are special benefits for women in the Referral approach. A study performed recently by Bernard Haldane Associates showed that business language or jargon is an area perceived as a hurdle by many women, especially those entering or re-entering the job market. The Referral interview is an excellent opportunity to gain knowledge and confidence in using the special language of a profession.

To summarize the experience of thousands of Haldane clients who have used this Referral approach, the actual job offers that resulted from the building of their personal contact networks came about as follows:

- First, contacts with whom clients had talked in the past days, weeks, or months later identified needs in their own organizations.
- Second, employers whom clients had never met, but who talked to a member of the clients' contact networks, learned about the clients and approached them to discuss opportunities. (A successful salesman once performed a study that convinced him that every time he talked to one

person he actually talked to seven people, six of them by proxy.)

- Third, clients were invited for a second meeting as a result of the initial meeting with one of their contacts, even though the clients did not expect to learn about an actual job opportunity, said so, and meant it.

There are also long-term benefits in the building and maintenance of a contact network, not only for your career, but for many other areas of your life. Many job and career seekers formed lifelong friendships with some of the people in their contact networks. It is always important to remember that real value can come only from an approach and attitude that is based on sincerity and a genuine concern for benefiting all parties involved. The moment this method is degraded to the level of a gimmick, or trick, it becomes useless. After all, none of us appreciates a trick being played on us, and we should have no wish to play tricks on others.

Some might say, "This looks like a very roundabout, long-winded way to find a job." There are two answers to this: First, we, the writers and readers of this book, are concerned with something more than getting work or getting a paycheck. Second, the experiences of many thousands of people who have used this method provide documented evidence that this approach *cuts in half* the time it takes to find a good job. Time spent on subsequent job and/or career changes is reduced even more dramatically. And the benefits in satisfaction and fulfillment, both in job and career terms, are incalculable. You will be tapping the most valuable resources available: your capacity and that of your fellow human beings to help each other.

Here are a number of common problems encountered by people in the beginning stages of a Referral campaign. These problems can be used as a troubleshooting list. All answers given here are solutions that have been successfully applied by job and career seekers:

Problem: I have just moved to this area; I don't know anyone here.

Solution: Start with the people you will do business with, such as the manager of the bank where you open your checking account. Include the people who will represent you in local, state, and federal government; important community leaders, such as clergymen, heads of civic organizations and chambers of commerce. They will see you whether they know you or not.

Problem: People say they are too busy to see me. I can't get in the door.

Solution: This usually means they have not understood your purpose or they feel you are asking them to find a job for you. Re-explain your purpose (in a letter or by phone). Assure them in so many words that you don't expect them to know of a job opening. Remember, busy people are the best contacts. Tell a busy person that you won't take more than twenty minutes of his or her time. Your *purposeful* persistence will be rewarded.

Problem: Interviewers suggest that there is no need to have a meeting. They want to chat by phone.

Solution: Explain that your career decision is one of the most important steps you will be taking in your life, and you won't be taking much of their time. Insist on a brief face-to-face meeting. The exception is a person who is about to go on a vacation or a business trip. Do the best you can on the telephone, observing all rules of a person-to-person interview. Then get the interviewer's return date, in order to set up a meeting after that time. Interviewers will be impressed with your strength of purpose.

Problem: I have tried to phone the person I want to see, and he or she has never returned my phone calls.

Solution: Again, busy people are the best interviewers. Many people have tried five to seven times before they made telephone contact. Persistence pays off! Make sure you have sent a letter clearly explaining your purpose. Avoid short-order cooking. Do not skip the letter and rely on your ability to explain your purpose on the telephone. Statistically, the success rate of this shortcut is very low.

Problem: I have a full-time job and can't take time off from work to conduct a Referral campaign.

Solution: The best contacts are senior-level professionals or executives. These people are rarely on a fixed time schedule. Their willingness to see you outside of normal business hours depends on your approach. Compare these two statements: "I can't take off from work, we'll have to set up a meeting in the evening" and "It would be unfair to my employer to interview on his time, and I know your time is valuable. If I make an effort, I could be at your office by 6 o'clock. Would you be able to see me briefly then?" Overwhelming evidence shows that this latter approach is almost always successful; Haldane clients have had no problem in setting up meetings during evenings, Saturdays, and even Sundays.

Problem: I can't seem to get through to my interviewers. They listen politely but never seem to be very helpful.

Solution: Chances are you do too much of the talking. We were given two ears and one mouth by nature and should use them in that proportion. Make sure your interviewer understands the purpose of the interview, as well as your job objective. Get his or her feedback by asking for it. Take a genuine interest in the interviewer. Also make sure you have a few questions prepared that you can ask the interviewer. If the interviewer doesn't know the answers, perhaps he or she can refer you to someone who does. Here are examples of such questions:

"I read in last Sunday's paper that XYZ (a company in your or your interviewer's career field) is building a new plant in our area. Do you know anything about them?"

"Can you advise me on the best sources of information in my chosen career field?" (in case of a career change); or, "What professional publications should I be reading?"

"I have tried to give the best examples of my work contributions in my resume; which ones would you advise me to expand on during my interviews?"

But, you may say at this point, why should I expose my ignorance on these subjects? The answer is that ignorance is never considered a sin, as long as it is accompanied by a genuine desire for enlightenment. Any sincere request for advice and information will always meet a positive response.

Problem: The interviewer advised me to change my job objective.

Solution: Here, listening carefully is especially important. Make sure you understand why an interviewer is making this suggestion. Ask questions! The interviewer may talk from personal experience, or you may come across as being unsure of your objective. You may need to explain why you chose your particular job and career objective.

If *three* or more interviewers make this same suggestion, consider revising your objective. In any case, be appreciative of the advice offered. After all, the interviewer is demonstrating a genuine interest in you and is likely to be an excellent link in your contact network.

Problem: The interviewer suggested rewriting my resume.

Solution: Same as above.

Problem: The interviewer asked: "How much money do you expect to make?"

Solution: This is a golden opportunity. Turn the question around and ask: "Based on your knowledge of me, I'd be interested in your evaluation of what I'm worth. How much should I be looking for?"

Problem: The interviewer told me I didn't have enough experience, or the right experience, for this job objective.

Solution: Another golden opportunity. Your attitude and response should be like this: "I'm glad I came to you; this is the kind of information I was looking for! *I know that my objective is right for me!* What steps would you advise me to take to get the experience necessary to carry it out?"

Problem: I'm told the job market is very tight in my field.

Solution: A "tight" job market means a "highly competitive" job market. Because most job seekers are ill prepared for a purposeful market campaign, you are likely to have the competitive edge. You will usually be the first to know when there *is* an opportunity.

Problem: There are *no* jobs in my field.

Solution: Same as above. As long as there are people *doing* a job, there *is* a job, by definition. The statement simply means that there are no "open" jobs, or that the interviewer does not *know* of any job vacancies. With an active contact network, a positive and determined attitude, and a clear objective, a tight job market is never a deterrent.

Problem: I can't get any referrals.

Solution: A request for a referral to another person must be preceded by complete rapport with the interviewer. If you have a problem getting your interviewer involved in what you are doing, if you have trouble getting feedback, advice, and information during interviews, work on those areas first, *before* you tackle the referral area. When you ask for referrals, make sure your interviewer knows that you are not asking for job leads. Say it in so many words. Give specific reasons, as described in this chapter, for wanting a referral. But also remember that not all your interviews have to result in referrals. Some can be very productive without referrals, and some of those even produce referrals later on.

Problem: The interviewer says he or she doesn't know anyone.

Solution: Same as above. This can be code language, meaning that the interviewer feels uncomfortable about referring you to people he or she knows. Or it can mean that the interviewer can't think of anyone at the moment. Try the "deferred" method described in this chapter. You might also bring to the interview a list of ten organizations in your field, which you heard or read about. Ask your interviewer to review this list. He or she may know something about some of these organizations that might be useful for you. He or she may even know one or two people in some of these organizations.

Problem: I have heard or read about a person I want to make contact with, but I have no referral to that person.

Solution: The first step is always a review of all your contacts for a possible direct or indirect referral to the person you want to see. However, if this is not possible, and timing is such that you can't wait for a referral, you can contact such a person directly by writing a "cold" Referral letter (described in the following chapter) explaining the reasons for wanting to meet the person. The success rate of setting up an interview by using this approach is slightly lower than by way of a personal referral. But you will have a reasonable chance of setting up the meeting, provided you have a good reason and state it well.

For many people who have gone from one job interview to the next, the very idea of interviews is depressing and conjures up visions of wasted time and personal hurt. The number of successful interviews seems to be far outnumbered by the number of unsuccessful ones. After a certain amount of such job interviewing, a feeling of rejection builds up, which poses a serious morale problem and makes it difficult for job seekers to look and feel their best.

The big advantage of a Referral campaign is that it consists only of successful interviews. Because you go into every interview with genuine, achievable purposes, you are never rejected. You always come out of the interview richer than you went in.

And as you become richer in terms of new, mutually beneficial relationships and valuable information, your morale and your excitement grow. Increasingly, your mental attitude and physical appearance reflect this enrichment. This is a major factor in the success Haldane clients experience in using the Referral method.

The following is an example of such a Referral campaign: Martin B. was a competent optical engineer who saw his career take a downturn as the company that employed him lost one contract after another. The decline of his company was accompanied by a decline in the national economy, and his hopes of building a career in the optical field diminished daily. But Martin knew that his ideal career was in optics and that nothing else would ever satisfy him to the same degree. He decided to seek professional help and give it one more good try.

Martin had not kept in touch with the field of optics, because his work had kept him so busy he had had very little time even with his family. His first three contacts were his tax accountant, a former employer whom Martin had always respected professionally, and his family doctor. Not having had experience with the Referral method, Martin reluctantly wrote to his three primary contacts, describing his situation. His first pleasant surprise came when all of them not only agreed to talk with him but congratulated him on his determination to re-establish his career. The tax accountant knew lit-

tle about the optical field but had made a specialty of working with people who were starting their own businesses. He
referred Martin to a man who had recently started a company
in the relatively new field of fiber optics.

The former employer not only gave him valuable information about recent developments in the optical field of which
Martin had been unaware, but referred him to three people.
One of these referrals was the president of an optical company that had been able to buck the negative trend of the
field by developing special competence in sophisticated new
optical techniques.

The family doctor said he wanted to help and eventually
provided one key referral.

At this point Martin's entire attitude had reversed itself. Instead of feeling that he was at the tail end of a losing situation, he now felt he was at the front end of a winning one.
This attitude impressed his interviewers, who became, in effect, an active sales force on his behalf. Martin's awareness of
the few successful people in an otherwise declining field became sharp and current. His campaign produced twenty-six
referrals and three job offers. Today Martin is executive vice-
president of an optical research firm. He is still in touch with
most of the contacts he made during his Referral campaign
and feels they have helped him to stay ahead in a competitive
field.

The glue that holds together the contact-making process is
communications. The next chapter expands this discussion
into written communications.

7
Building Communications

Communications are an integral part of job and career strategy. No piece of paper can ever take the place of a face-to-face interview, but letters, resumes, and telephone calls are the starting points on the road to an interview. Developing your communicating skills will enable you to construct bridges between you and your interviewers. If you can design a good resume, write effective letters, and communicate by telephone, you will have a competitive edge in your market campaign. This chapter will give you ground rules for successful resume and letter writing, as well as telephone techniques.

The purpose of this book is to help you to understand and apply proven methods for finding *your* job and building *your* career. No resume or letter written by another person, however competently, is going to fit your needs. No standard style or format is going to serve your purpose. Therefore, you will not find prefabricated examples of such documents in this chapter. You will, however, be guided, paragraph by paragraph, through the construction of your own tailor-made letters and resumes.

All your written and verbal communications have one thing in common: They show your interviewers and employers that you know who you are and where you are going. The style, content, and appearance of your written communications say as much about you as the clothes you wear to an interview, and they need to be chosen with the same care.

The resume-writing field is flooded with do's and don'ts. Between them they cover all the possibilities, from never using a resume at all to writing a five-page curriculum vitae, complete with picture of smiling family and date of grandmother's birth.

Resumes don't get jobs. People get jobs.

But it is essential that you write a resume, for the following reasons: The process of compiling a resume will make you review and focus your assets, put them in order, and fine-tune them for presentation to an interviewer. Even if you were never to use the finished product, it would be necessary to go through this step in order to prepare yourself for a market campaign.

A good resume, if it is constructed and used properly, can be a major factor in getting an interview. During the interview it can serve as an agenda. As long as both you and your interviewer are talking about the subjects highlighted on the resume, you will look and sound good. A well-organized documentation of your abilities is always an asset during an interview.

The customary resume format is chronological. It is outmoded. The chronological format highlights employment dates, which are listed prominently on the left side of the resume. The dates attract the eye and lead the reader to leap to instant conclusions based on personal prejudices regarding the proper length of time a person should hold a job. Many resumes don't survive this operation and wind up in the wastebasket prematurely. The chronological format is nothing but a bad habit, regardless of the number of people who subscribe to it, and it is geared only to the work pattern of overworked, professional resume scanners.

Responsible decision makers want to know *what* you did and how *well* you did it. *When* you did it runs a poor third. Most conventional resumes never give any information on the quality of a person's work and the results the person got. True, even a well-written resume is no proof of anything by itself, but is more likely to lead to an interview during which the information it gives can be verified.

A number of people advise that you produce a new resume for each interview. They suggest that you tailor your resume, and yourself along with it, to a situation about which you have no firsthand knowledge. This advice is based on a basic misunderstanding of how the job-finding process works. It is indeed necessary to get on your interviewers' wavelength, but only after you have met, listened to, and understood them— never by abandoning your success pattern and career objective as stated on your resume. (There is one exception: *After* a first interview for a job, the interviewer may request a more detailed written presentation that relates your specific experience and abilities to the organization's needs.)

A resume must be future-oriented. An employer can only "hire your future," not your past. The past is relevant only insofar as it shows your potential for the future. The word "resume" itself sounds like a contradiction in terms, because it deals with the past. The word is retained here only for purposes of easy communication.

Your resume must reflect your uniqueness. Your combined assets, abilities, talents, experience, and education are not like anyone else's. An average, run-of-the-mill resume implies that you are an average, run-of-the-mill person. Be in control of what you put in your resume and what you leave out.

Put your best foot forward. Interviewers don't want to know what you *can't* do. They want to know what you *can* do. At the same time, any inflation of the facts will get in your way later. You will be asked to prove what you say in your resume. Words like "more than," "over," "etc.," tend to weaken a statement because they are perceived as attempts to inflate statements or figures. "Saved my company $10,000" sounds stronger than "Saved my company more than $10,000."

One of the resume functions is to build a bridge between you and your interviewers. As in every other facet of job and career building, keep the human factor in mind. Besides using clear and concise language that is easily read and understood by a reader, think in terms of contributing to an employer's organization at the same time you meet your own needs. One without the other is nonproductive. An easy way to satisfy this condition is to include your employers in the phrasing of your job objective: Let the reader of your resume know what you expect to contribute to your future employer's organization (in general terms) and what you have contributed to your past employers (in specific terms).

For instance: If your job objective is sales, state that your skill and experience in sales will result in a sales increase. Demonstrate that this is a realistic expectation by giving examples of past sales achievements later on in your resume. Every prospective employer will react favorably to your stated intentions to produce results. And part of your resume will be devoted to listing past results.

Include information relevant to your job objective only. Leave out all other information, however interesting it might be. Resist the temptation to include something for everyone. It will only make you appear to be a jack-of-all-trades and a master of none. Leave out all negative information, or information that could be interpreted negatively. You can supply such information during an interview, if it is requested. At that time you will be in control, and you can demonstrate a positive attitude with regard to the information.

There are only two absolute requirements in a resume: one,

a statement of purpose, and two, proof that you are capable of accomplishing that purpose. Remember this throughout the process of writing a resume.

Your objective is the most important part of your resume. It is a statement of purpose and must gain the reader's immediate and positive attention.

Writing a statement of your job and career objectives will give you an opportunity to develop clear and concise language. Start by writing down your job objective as it has been developed up to this point. This should include your major areas of strength, combined in a strong and positive statement that reflects your thoughts and feelings about what you want to do.

It is often preferable to express your job objective in terms of job functions and not in terms of job titles. However, if you wish to use a job title, remember that you share this title with thousands of others, and the reader of your resume will still want to know what makes you unique.

Focus on your greatest areas of strength and motivation. Refrain from listing *all* your abilities and interests. This will only weaken your statement.

The following are examples of three different job objectives, using different styles:

Job Objective: To assume responsibility for the processing of information, to improve existing administrative systems, and to initiate, develop, and implement effective new systems.

OBJECTIVE: To communicate an organization's purpose to the public. Successful experience in verbal, written, and graphic communications, skill in dealing with people at all levels, and a structured approach to problem solving will contribute to projecting an organization's image of effectiveness.

CAREER OBJECTIVE

Industrial Relations Management:

Where successful experience in all phases of personnel administration, together with proven leadership ability and communication skills, results in the design and implementation of cost-effective personnel policies.

The qualifications section of the resume is a brief, concise summary of the major areas of experience and accomplishment offered in support of your job objective. This information may be given in narrative style or in single words or terms, but it must be brief, clear, and easy to scan.

Qualifications:
> ten years' experience in sales
> supervision and training of manufacturer's agents and distributor salesmen
> pricing, gross margin control, and distribution
> sales promotion, advertising, and trade shows
> new product development

Qualified by:
> a record of increasing management responsibility involving control and supervision, the development of new products and packages and the successful repositioning of existing products

The strongest support you can give to your job objective is a selection of achievements. They prove that your job objective is realistic.

As a rule of thumb, give two strong specific examples in support of each of the areas of strength you listed in your job objective. Make sure the words and phrases you use relate clearly to the job objective.

Achievements should be listed separately from the experience section of your resume. They might otherwise be confused with your past job descriptions. Given a choice, most readers will pay more attention to specific accomplishments than job descriptions, which are generally considered dull reading. Make sure you use simple, concise language, and give results. *"Accomplishments," "Related Achievements," "Results"* or *"Examples of Effectiveness."*

Accomplishments:

Coordinated the development and introduction of two new product lines that achieved $500,000 in sales. Achieved new sales highs and significant profit improvement for a product originally developed in the mid-1800s, by developing a new way to position and sell it.

Set up a complete accounting system. Resulted in accurate cost accounting information and reconciliation of discrepancies.

Created and presented three-hour mixed media production which resulted in a 12 percent increase over the previous year in funds raised by a social service organization.

A good way to lead the reader's eye to a series of accomplishments that highlight one of your areas of strength is to combine and label related accomplishments.

Training and Motivating:

Revitalized photographic department, training inexperienced photographers to produce exciting, award-winning work. Originated innovative printing procedures and techniques.

Developed unique method to teach graphic design, encouraging both speed and creativity.

The experience section of your resume relates your employment history. Starting either with the most recent, or with the most relevant to your job objective, list your job title, your employer/company, a brief description of the major functions or duties of your job, and the dates of employment (years only).

If any of your former job titles do not accurately reflect your responsibility in those jobs, use functional titles. For instance, if your title was "Sales Representative," but you actually were also responsible for training salespeople, give your title as "Sales and Sales Training."

In describing your past job, emphasize those duties that relate directly to your job objective. They are the ones in which the reader is interested.

If the employment dates appear to give negative information about you, leave them out. It is better to be asked to supply dates in person, when you can explain seeming discrepancies, than to be screened out in advance by people who don't like the dates as given on your resume.

Experience

> TERRITORY MANAGER, Acme Carpets; Division of ABC Industries, Smithfield, IL. Responsible for all aspects of company operations and policy within territory. Analyzed, planned, and implemented sales operations and marketing strategy (1967 to 1975).

> VOCATIONAL-AGRICULTURAL INSTRUCTOR. Joliet County Technical School, Joliet, FL. Trained students in crop and livestock production. Trained students in agricultural mechanics. Managed student organizational funds amounting to $15,000. Planned yearly and weekly training schedules. Requisitioned $7,000 worth of tools and supplies prior to use (1979 to present).

If many of your jobs were irrelevant to your job objective, you can write a brief summary paragraph giving highlights of your experience as it relates to your job objective, as well as the total period of time covering these activities. For example:

Experience

Twelve years of professional experience in all phases of personnel training and development. Set up a variety of training and motivational programs. Created new approaches to employee motivation (1968 to present). You may then list your employers for that period of time

Employers

United States Army

Manufacturers Mutual Insurance Corporation, Bellville, MA.

When giving information about your education, list your highest degree first. Add nonacademic education and training if it is relevant to your job objective.

Education

M. Ed., Education and Human Values, Brighton College

B.S. in Mathematics, University of Birmingham

Graduate Studies in Business Administration, Brighton College

If you feel that you have the equivalent of academic certification in terms of training and experience, and can give data for it, consider listing such an equivalent on your resume.

Education

B.BA. in Accounting (equiv.) through studies at Bromley College, Stanton, IA, as well as 12 years of related business experience.

If your education relates directly to your job objective, list it in the second or third place on your resume. If not, place it near the end. In most cases, the dates of your degrees do not supply relevant information and should be left out.

Include other supporting data—relevant memberships, awards, publications, patents—only if they support your job objective. In some cases, avocations relate to job objectives and may be listed, but more often they become relevant only during interviews. When you recognize that you and the interviewer have a common interest, you can mention your interest or avocation as a means of establishing closer rapport with him or her.

Professional Affiliations
Member of Bar, Illinois and Iowa;
Chicago Bar Association, 1971-1978.

Awards
First Prize, 1976 Cayuga Art Show.

Special award, Boston Arts Festival, 1979.

Also, consider listing the following personal data: age, marital status, and children; but make sure that the information you give cannot be interpreted negatively. "When in doubt, leave it out!" You will be in a more favorable position during the interview to give some of this information. If you are not sure about giving your age, don't give it; if your health is not excellent, don't mention it.

Personal
Age 48. Married, 2 children. Excellent health.

or:

Personal
Married, no children.

At the end of your resume, add anything of relevance that you wish the reader to know. (Never include references in your resume. It's premature.)

> Supporting materials available during interview.
> Willing to relocate.

Recheck all the information in your resume to make sure it supports your job objective. Trim all unnecessary words.

Decide on the format you would like to use. One-page resumes tend to be strongest. If you have more than ten years of experience, you may need two pages. A resume of more than two pages is frequently ineffective: You are then relying on the busy reader to do his own editing, and you thereby lose control.

Any resume can be edited down to two pages or less. A study performed some years ago showed that the average person expends 60 percent of his energy on reading the first page of a resume, 30 percent on the second page, and you can see how much is left for the following pages. This also shows that the most important information should be on page one. If your accomplishments are your strongest feature, place them on the first page, ahead of your experience. If your work history and past titles tell an impressive story, put *them* ahead of the other sections.

Arrange all the information you have developed in order of its importance and try various layouts to determine which has the best appearance and impact.

Make use of spacing, capital letters, and underlining to direct the reader's eye to the most important and strongest statements on your resume.

Put your name, address, and telephone number in a place on the resume where they can be easily seen.

Just as you would always go on an interview dressed neatly and conservatively, you should own a resume you can be proud of, one that has been professionally typeset or photo-composed, and printed on one or two pages of high-quality, fairly heavy paper. Remember, a good-looking resume will still cost you considerably less than the clothing you are wearing to your interview. And the trouble you took to prepare your resume will be one more reassuring fact, one more accomplishment in your interviewer's eyes.

The best way to use your resume is to target it carefully. An indiscriminate mass mailing produces only waste and disappointment.

Here are some ground rules about the proper use of resumes:

Every person you intend to talk with during your market campaign must have advance information about you. If you ask a busy person to give you time and attention, it is only a matter of courtesy to provide information about yourself in preparation for the interview. It also gives structure to the interview.

Combine a strong and positive resume with a letter (described below) that relates a request for a meeting to the interests of the interviewer and you will almost always be granted the interview.

It is always wise to carry one or more copies of your resume with you wherever you go. Opportunities for making valuable contacts arise at the most unexpected times. However, if you find yourself without it, you can always mail one to your contact later.

Your resume should be a "living" document. Update it at least once a year. If you find that you have no new accomplishments to add, your career may have gone into a period of stagnation. Review your career objectives and the progress you have made, if any, during the past year.

The design and preparation of effective letters are as vital to your job and career strategy as a strong and positive resume. The reasons for writing any letter are to establish a link with another person, to communicate a purpose or point of view, and to initiate future action—to get results.

There are two aspects of writing a letter: format and content. And every letter you write will say something about you as a person. The people who haven't met you will make judgments about you from the appearance and legibility of your letters, while people who know you will judge your seriousness of purpose by your letters.

In terms of format, letters written as part of a job search are in the true sense business letters and should have a business-like appearance. Although well-designed, personalized stationery can be effective, it is the attitude conveyed by the letter that counts, not necessarily the money spent on it. Good, heavier-than-normal letter paper is not expensive. If colored paper is used, it should be only slightly off-white. Size is not important, but extremes should be avoided. Tiny or extra-large formats irritate many recipients.

Except for thank-you letters to people with whom you have a personal relationship, all letters should be typed. Everyone can have access to a typewriter or to a person who can type letters. If nothing else, a neatly typed letter is a courtesy to the reader. And be sure the type face is clean. Dirty type can ruin the entire effect and completely wipe out the effort that went into composing a good letter.

The layout of a business letter is a matter of fashion. Your best way to learn how to set up a letter on a page is to study a few examples of recent business letters and pick the format that most appeals to you.

Make sure you spell the addressee's name right. If he or she has a title, find out what it is. You can usually inquire at his or her company or organization. Failure to do this is like saying "I don't know or care about you!"

Now that you have cleared the hurdle of getting the recipient into a receptive frame of mind by first observing the ground rules about format, we come to the most important aspect of any letter: the content. Your task is to establish a communications link with the recipient.

You have heard that a business letter should be brief, clear, and to the point. What is just as important is that your letters be warm and personal.

In fact, the real art of writing a good letter is to strike a fine balance between crispness and warmth. This takes practice. Imagine, for example, that you are writing a letter to a person whose article in last Sunday's newspaper you read and liked. You could acknowledge having read the article by saying, "I read your article." That's crisp. Or you could say, "I found your article interesting." Very little enthusiasm here! How about: "I enjoyed reading your article" or even "I enjoyed reading your fine article." You have just made someone feel good about you!

Here is an excellent way to write a good letter when you have had little practice: Think about what you want to say, and what you want the letter to accomplish. Most letters are like arrows shot into the air. Few people think through the purpose of their letters, and they are usually disappointed by the responses they get. The response has to be built into a letter before it is sent.

Write an outline of your key ideas, then write a first draft of your letter quickly and in the language you use every day. Then edit the letter, taking out all unnecessary words, making sure it is concise as well as warm. You want your feelings to come through along with your thoughts. After some practice, you'll develop a natural style, and your letters will need very little editing.

The most difficult letter to write is a letter asking for an interview. (It makes no sense to write a letter asking for a job,

because every job offer is preceded by at least one interview.)
Here is a method for designing such a letter:

The first paragraph must build the bridge between you and
the reader, especially if you don't know the person to whom
you are writing. An acknowledgment of the person's position
or accomplishments will usually serve this purpose. Example:
"I'm writing to you because of your position as a leader in our
community," or: "Reading your fine book on . . . prompted
me to write you this letter." Most people have a professional
position, and all people have accomplishments of which they
are proud. It takes very little research to get this information.

Incidentally, don't be afraid to start a letter or an occasional
sentence with "I." This phobia is one of the many taboos responsible for the flood of artificial and stilted business letters
sent every day. Unless it is carried to extremes, starting a sentence with "I" in your letters is taken as a sign of self-confidence by most interviewers, even though from a stylistic point
of view it may seem objectionable.

If the letter is written to a person you have been referred
to, say: "Mr./Ms. X (the person who provided you with the referral) suggested I write to you"; or more warmly: "Mr./Ms.
X spoke very highly of you and suggested that I get in touch
with you."

At this point, it is important to note that getting information about the person you are writing to is very easy when you
have been referred to him or her by someone else. The information is literally available for the asking. It will enable you
to open your letter on a much stronger and more personal
note.

The opening paragraph should be followed by a clear statement of your purpose. (Don't keep the reader in suspense. He
may not last until the end!) Examples: "At this point in my career I need to make a decision, and I'd like to ask your ad-

vice." Or: "I would like to meet you in person, at a time convenient for you." Make sure you give reasons that clearly explain your purpose.

If the recipient does not know you, you should give some information about yourself in the next paragraph. Again, this is a courtesy to the reader and should include a reference to the resume you are enclosing, which will add to the information given in the letter.

Unless you know that the person to whom you are writing has a job opening, and you are applying for that position, make a firm statement at this point that you are *not* expecting him or her to know of a current job opening. This will take the pressure off your potential interviewer and make it possible for him or her to meet you without being obligated to consider you for a job. As described in detail in the chapter on contacts, this must be done with absolute sincerity.

The last paragraph of your letter initiates action. What would you like to happen as a result of writing the letter? What would you like the recipient to do? The only way you can be sure that anything will happen is to take the initiative yourself.

Many people have reached old age waiting for a response to letters that ended: "I look forward to hearing from you." It is both unreasonable and discourteous to put the burden of action or follow-through on the recipients of your letters. An example of a good ending is "I will call you in a few days to discuss this further with you." Or: "I will telephone you on Monday to find out when we can meet." Or: "I will call you next week to get your reaction to . . ."

The salutation and the closing are very much a matter of personal preference, but there is one important rule: No letter related to a job search should ever begin with "Dear Sir" or "Gentlemen." There is always a way of finding out the name of a person you can write to. Your search for a job, or other

serious enterprise, requires that you carefully target each letter and avoid sending "confetti" letters.

One of the most competitive approaches to the job market
involves using help wanted advertising. There are two types
of job ads: "blind" ads and "company" ads.

In the blind ad, the advertiser is identified only by a box
number. Unless you have special inside knowledge that allows
you to identify the company that placed the ad from the information given in the ad, you won't be able to address your
response to a specific person.

The other and more desirable type of ad is the company ad,
where the advertiser is identified in the body of the copy.
When answering a company ad, your response can be targeted more specifically, and you can follow it up by telephone.

In either case often hundreds of people respond to the same
ad, and the company that placed it is flooded with letters. It
soon becomes physically impossible for anyone to read all
those letters and study all those resumes.

You can, therefore, assume that your response to a want ad
will get the recipient's attention for a few seconds only. With
that in mind, you can do a number of things to maximize
your results.

Write a "quick-response letter" with a positive statement:
"I have read your ad in the (name of newspaper). I have the
qualifications necessary for doing the job." Or: "In answer to
your ad in (name of newspaper), I feel I am qualified for the
position of...." Any doubt about your ability to do the job
should not show up in your letter; it may eliminate you at the
start. If you are in doubt about whether or not you would like
the job, keep it to yourself. You will always have the chance to
turn the job down after you have been made an offer.

The second paragraph of your letter should be a clear, easy-
to-read-at-a-glance description of the match between the employer's needs and your abilities. Divide the paragraph into

two columns. On the left side of the paper write the three or four most important requirements listed in the ad. On the right side list your corresponding qualifications. Include experience, education, or special training.

Your Requirements:	*My Qualifications:*
5 years of management-level experience	3 years as Personnel Manager plus 2½ years as Vice President of Industrial Relations
Knowledge of wage and salary administration	7 years experience in all aspects of personnel administration, including wage and salary and employee benefits
Business degree	B.B.A., Southeastern University
Labor negotiations experience	Successfully negotiated three contracts with national union, avoiding major confrontations and strikes

If you lack the required education or experience, state that you have the equivalent in actual accomplishments, and list them. Make sure that for each accomplishment you list, you also give a result. This will make it believable. Use a "telegram-style" in order to save the reader time: "Supervised $500,000 construction project; completed project within time and budget limits."

Accomplishments don't always have to be big to show that you are qualified to do a job. What is important is that they are specific, clear, and relevant to the job described in the ad.

If you are answering a blind ad, conclude the letter with a simple statement like this: "I am available for a personal interview," or: "I look forward to hearing from you." (In this case no personal follow-up by telephone is possible.) If the name of a person or a company is listed in the ad, it is not a blind ad and you can end the letter with: "I will call you in a few days to set up a meeting to discuss my qualifications."

If your resume relates directly to the job described in the ad, enclose it. If not, don't send it—it will only confuse the issue.

Do not give your salary requirements even if the advertisement requests them. Save this information for face-to-face salary negotiations.

You can see from the above that supreme self-confidence must be part of your approach. You can never tell whether or not you can do a job simply by reading a newspaper ad. You don't have enough information. But by using a self-confident approach, you demonstrate to the employer that you think well of yourself and have the determination and initiative to give the job your best effort. This doesn't guarantee you the job, but it will vastly improve your chances of getting an interview. Once you have an interview, you have covered half the distance toward getting the job offer.

Now comes the most important type of letter you will *ever* write: the thank-you letter.

How many thank-you letters have you received in the course of your career. A thousand? A hundred? Ten? Five? Chances are you remember most of them. And what's more, you remember them with pleasure. You probably showed them to friends and associates.

How many thank-you letters have you written to others?

Not only does it make you feel good to have received such a letter, it makes you feel good to write one. Here's another fact about thank-you letters that is not always recognized: They are the best means to get action; sometimes they can work miracles.

One of our clients recently wrote a thank-you letter to a company vice-president who had given him a cold, five-minute interview before dismissing him abruptly. The letter said, in summary, that our client understood the pressure the vice-president was under and, far from being annoyed, appreciated the time spent with him. This thank-you letter resulted in an invitation to another interview (this one lasted two hours) and eventually produced a job offer.

The ground rules for a thank-you letter are simple. Once again, it is well to stay away from stereotyped formats. Rather than say, "I found our last meeting interesting," express your feelings more directly, and say, "I enjoyed our meeting." Then explain why. Recall the occasion to the recipient's mind by recounting some of its highlights. This also shows that you paid attention, that the occasion was important to you.

One aspect of the thank-you letter that most people overlook is the opportunity to initiate future action. When you thank a person for giving you an interview, describe the Next Step. This could be setting up a second interview or taking some action you promised during the interview. Every occasion that produces a thank-you letter is a step in a relationship with another person. There is always a Next Step.

The most difficult thank-you letters to write are the ones following a negative occasion, an indifferent or bad interview, or a turn-down for a job. These are also the most necessary times to write thank-you letters. A simple action like taking control of your own feelings and writing a friendly thank-you letter can be a dramatic testimonial to the power of positive thinking. Many of our clients have succeeded in turning around attitudes, and re-establishing positive and productive relationships. When you have been turned down for a job, it doesn't mean you have been forever rejected or eliminated from consideration by a person or an organization. A good thank-you letter can often put you back in the running for the next opportunity.

A client, Alan M., had been considered and then turned down for a position on the basis that the company's board of directors had upgraded the position and offered it to a person with experience far superior to Alan's.

He reacted with disappointment and understandable anger at the company's sudden reversal. He felt sure they had been dishonest with him, and he was never going to talk to them again. After Alan had time to reconsider, he decided to take a more rational approach. He wrote a letter to the president of the company expressing his thanks for having been considered for the job, and congratulating the president on his decision. Alan also asked for another meeting to discuss what contributions he could make to the company in view of the new policy they had decided on. The interview was freely granted, and it developed that the policy change on the company's part was due to some advice Alan had given the president during an earlier interview.

Alan's credentials were very solid, but the president had been too embarrassed to offer him an inferior position. As a result of this meeting, an associate position was created, which carried more scope and salary than the one originally offered. Alan M. is convinced that none of this would have been possible had he not written his thank-you letter to the president.

This is not an isolated example; the power of positive thank-you letters is incredible. It may not move mountains, but it certainly moves people, and there is nothing mysterious about it.

When a thank-you letter is written as part of your job, or during a search for one, it is still a business letter and should be typed. Only people with whom you have a personal relationship should receive handwritten thank-you letters.

Throughout your working life, any contact with another person, other than daily routine, is a cause for writing a thank-you letter. Some of the busiest and most senior people in the business world are known for writing thank-you letters for the thank-you letters they receive!

When should you write a thank-you letter? "When in doubt, write a thank-you letter!"

Sometimes the job you are looking for exists in the organization that currently employs you. The ground rules for resume and letter writing described above will apply, with certain modifications, to such a situation. The specialized written materials needed for your employer will be discussed step by step in Chapter 13, "The Internal Campaign."

Special kinds of letters are also required whenever you wish to relocate to another part of the country. This process, and the letters needed for it, are described in Chapter 11, "The Long-Distance Campaign."

In addition to letter writing, telephone communications are an ever-present part of a market campaign. Here are some general rules:

Before you pick up the telephone to make a call, think about your purpose. If it is something other than a routine call, make some notes on a piece of paper to serve as a guide during your conversation. And as strange as it may sound, posture is an important aspect of an effective telephone technique. Invariably a person sitting up straight or leaning forward slightly sounds more purposeful than a person leaning back in a comfortable chair. The number of interview appointments obtained by our clients who followed this simple rule proves this beyond a doubt.

As with every other type of communication, results are achieved by building rapport between two people. I once conducted a seminar on communications where one participant requested information on any "tricks" he could use to "get past the secretary" in making an appointment with a senior executive. Before I had a chance to answer, another participant said, "I can give you the best trick of all: Treat her like a human being!" It's that simple.

The important but sometimes difficult kind of phone call is

the one made as a follow-up to a letter asking for an interview. Be sure to go out of your way to establish rapport with secretaries or receptionists, who are facilitators and valuable business contacts. When talking to an executive's secretary, be firm and positive without seeming arrogant. If you appear hesitant or unsure of yourself, you may be put on the defensive, and your chances of getting to talk with the person you are calling are minimized. *Expect* to get through and to get the interview.

If asked the nature of your call by the secretary, say that you have sent a letter that explains your purpose, and your call is expected. Ask to speak with the executive. If pressed further, explain your purpose briefly, as you stated it in your letter. If you have been referred to the executive, explain that Mr./Ms. X, the V.P. of the ABC Corporation, has suggested that you talk with the executive in order to seek his or her comment on and reaction to the information you have sent in your letter.

If the executive is out, or otherwise unavailable, find out the best time to call back, or ask if the secretary can set up the appointment. Retain the initiative. Do not wait to be called back. It is also advisable to get the secretary's name, because you will be calling back, and there may be more than one person answering the phone.

When you talk with the executive, identify yourself and immediately explain your purpose. Again, if you have been referred, say that Mr./Ms. X has suggested you talk with him or her. This referral may be the only link you have with the executive. Now is the time to stress it. State that you sent a letter and ask if the executive has had a chance to read it. If so, mention two specific appointment dates and hours that are convenient for you. Have your appointment book available. Don't say, "I am available anytime"; it makes you look disorganized and inactive. The executive will either agree to one of your times or suggest an alternative. Do not at this point begin a long explanation about the reason for your call. Your letter has explained your purpose.

If your letter has not been received or read, in most cases it is best to offer to call back the next day. If the letter has not been received by then, send a copy and follow through in the normal way. In a very few instances, you may choose to explain your purpose verbally over the telephone, but this is frequently difficult when the executive has not seen your letter. End by indicating your enthusiasm for the planned meeting.

Never conduct an interview over the phone.

Cut the conversation short, and indicate that you are looking forward to meeting the interviewer in person. Telephone interviews normally lead nowhere, because the lack of face-to-face contact prevents you from carrying out the first purpose of any interview: establishing rapport with the interviewer.

The best kind of interviewer is a very busy person. Busy people are active, involved, and usually knowledgeable. You can get more information from such a person than from a dozen others. A busy person is also hard to get to, so you may have to make many telephone calls to set up an interview. It is not unusual to make seven to ten tries before you connect. In most cases, the investment in time and effort pays off.

It's like the story Victor Borge tells about the man who invented a soft drink called one-up. It didn't sell, so he invented two-up, then three-up, etc. When six-up wasn't successful, he gave up. Little did he know how close he came!

One method of follow-up, when a person is difficult to reach by telephone, is to write a positive letter saying that you understand the other person's time problem, and you will make it easier by calling at a certain day and time. Assure the person that your call will take only a few moments. Our clients have been successful most often using this approach.

When making any kind of follow-up telephone call, be positive. If you complain about not having been called back or about having difficulty reaching a person, you will not be successful.

Some telephone calls are made in order to get information. You may want to get the correct name or title of a person you intend to write to. You may want to get facts about a company or its products. In every case a firm but polite approach combined with the expectation of being successful will help you get results.

It is human nature to want to meet expectations when they are positively stated. If the person with whom you are talking doesn't have the information, ask for another source from which you can get it. Learning how to make telephone calls with ease will give you confidence that your expectations will be met. This, in turn, will increase your chances of success.

Effective communication requires on-the-job training. Practice it often! Remember, there is no need to be particularly outgoing or aggressive. All it takes is a firm purpose every time you initiate communication with someone. And constant practice.

Up to this point, we have discussed the different elements of a market campaign. Now let's discuss how you can put them all together.

8
The Market Campaign

You will be as successful in your career as you expect to be, provided your expectations are firmly based on your Success Factors. The same is true for finding your next job.

Over a period of thirty years, all of our clients who fully expected and intended to be successful have reached their objective.

A *market campaign* is the purposeful activity that leads to a job and significant career advancement. A successful market campaign depends on two other factors: the quality of your planning, and your enthusiasm for the adventure you are about to embark on, the exploration of the various options open to you in the world of work. This enthusiasm can come only from clear knowledge of what it takes to make your next job an exciting and fulfilling one.

Job market conditions are a minor factor, because the method described here for planning and conducting a market campaign, based on an informed view of the real world, enables you to deal with any and all conditions you will find in the job market.

Here are the ground rules for planning a successful market campaign.

Make each step in your campaign achievable. A successful

campaign can be based only on successful actions, not on failures. The difference between success and failure consists of realistic expectations. For example, if every interview is expected to result in a job offer, then most of them will be failures.

One of the purposes of every interview is to get useful information and to add to your knowledge of the work world in general and your career field in particular. This expectation can be met at every interview. Knowledge builds confidence. When you have had a series of successful interviews, you will think, act, and look like a successful person, and you will be much more likely to be offered a job than the average job seeker, who is tossed about on the sea of chance and luck.

None of us achieves anything in this world without the help of others. The recognition of this fact of life is *the most important factor* in achieving job and career success.

This is not to say that you will turn control over to other people and expect them to do the job for you. But if you have a purpose, and a plan for achieving it, the help and support you get from others will become an important part of your market campaign and your career.

Before you actually begin your market campaign, give careful thought to planning your time. A job search based on the principle of "looking around, just in case a job comes up" can have a very negative effect on your state of mind. As a way to stay in touch with the job market, it has value, but it cannot be expected to produce the same results as a purposeful market campaign. Because "looking around" does not usually result in a series of job offers, and frequently produces none at all, it may lead you to uninformed, unrealistic conclusions regarding the number and type of job opportunities in your field. It may also make you feel that no one really wants you.

A well-planned market campaign, with a purpose and the

expectation of success, will produce results. Our 55,000 past clients, plus new ones every day, are living proof of this fact.

Plan your market campaign as an activity using eight hours a day, five days a week and sometimes Saturdays, too. A successful market campaign is a full-time job, and you will work harder at it than at most jobs you have ever held.

But any job is impossible to do if you have to create it over again every day. In order to be able to work productively you will have to set up a structure. Information on the job market provided in Chapter 5 tells you that at least two-thirds of your time will be reserved for the "informal" or Referral approach, which involves making and following up contacts. The remaining one-third or less will be spent in the advertised or published job market. The exact proportions depend on your job and career field, and how job information is transmitted in that field.

When conducting a market campaign is your current full-time employment, treat it as you would any other full-time employment. Get up at your normal time, dress as you would for work. Over the years you have developed habits that enable you to see yourself in a framework of productive and rewarding work. There is every reason to continue working within this framework.

After a few days of start-up activity, mostly devoted to resumes and letters, you should expect to have two interviews every day of the week. At this rate you will build up a momentum that will be one of the major factors in the response you receive. Whatever your technical qualifications for a job, interviewers will always gravitate to you if you are purposeful and active. Everyone likes to give support to positively active people. Such people produce results and are likely to act on our advice. They are also a credit to us when we refer them to others. This, incidentally, is the reason why, during your market campaign, referrals to others or invitations for second interviews are a real measure of how you appear to your interviewers.

How and when do you schedule interviews if you are working in a job with fixed hours? This is an important question, and the answer has been documented by thousands of our clients who have conducted successful market campaigns while being productive in their jobs.

When you are employed, you will need to reduce the time you spend on your market campaign without, at the same time, diluting it. Two to three interviews per week are a realistic expectation. Some interviews can be scheduled on Saturdays, and Sundays can be reserved for answering ads and writing letters.

Remember, the busy executive at the decision-making level is the best of all possible interviewers. Such a person usually does not punch a time clock, literally or figuratively, and it is relatively simple to set up evening or Saturday interviews. The approach you use when you ask someone to see you outside of normal business hours must be based on an understanding of good human relations practices. The wrong way to ask for an evening interview is to say, "I can't come to see you during working hours; it will have to be in the evening." You will usually get a negative response. You can virtually ensure a positive response by saying (or writing) something like this: "I have a problem leaving work early, but I also know that you are very busy. If I hurry, I could be there by 5:30; I'll take up only a few minutes of your time. Would that be all right?" You have demonstrated that you are prepared to do your part in reducing inconvenience to the interviewer. Most people respond favorably to such an attitude.

It may be necessary to take some time out of your current job, especially when you have answered ads and are scheduled to talk to someone in a personnel department. Even in those cases, it is remarkable how many people are responsive to a request for an evening or Saturday interview. But the first rule always is to give a full commitment and do a good job for your current employer. That and a positive attitude will relieve you of worry about a few hours taken off to advance your career.

It is your right to move ahead in your career—on the job if possible, but into another job if your current employer offers no chance for advancement. Your superiors have the same rights, and they will exercise them. But consider carefully the relative advantages and disadvantages of leaving a job in order to look for a new one. Although the problem of being unemployed can be overcome by conducting a concentrated, positive market campaign, the status of unemployment sometimes creates a hurdle in interviewers' minds. Unless there is an extreme problem in interpersonal relationships in your job, and a pervasive negative attitude resulting from it, I advise against leaving your present work before finding something new.

Another aspect of a market campaign to be considered is pacing. You will no more be able to sustain a seven-day-a-week market campaign than a seven-day-a-week job. Plan some time periodically to recharge your batteries. Include activities that you thoroughly enjoy. Your campaign will be as strong as your attitude. Positive feelings are generated by a combination of results and enjoyment. In everything you do, part of the enjoyment comes from avocational activities—the things you don't *have* to do.

One of my clients, Margery D., who had been on many interviews, complained of a lack of progress in her market campaign. She always received a good reception, but she was never invited back for a second interview. Finally one of her early interviewers, who happened to be a former client, called me and asked, "Does she have a health problem? She seems to be more in need of a vacation than a job."

Margery had been under great pressure from her mother not to let up. That, combined with a misplaced work ethic, kept her from taking so much as an hour off from her market campaign. She had no problem getting referrals and interviews, but that's as far as it went. With great difficulty I persuaded her to relax over a long weekend. She spent the weekend at the beach and came back tanned and full of energy. It took only three more interviews for her to receive her first job offer.

Periodically take part in activities that give you pleasure and restore your vigor. Every time you have accomplished something positive during your market campaign, give yourself a reward. Taking time off because you can't think of anything else to do, or don't feel like doing anything, reduces your momentum. Taking time off to reward yourself for successful activity increases it.

Another important aspect of preparing for a market campaign is your appearance. How do you dress for interviews? Rather than reading books on the subject, use and develop your powers of observation. Besides the general and ever-changing fashions of business clothes, many job and career environments have their own dress codes. Get a good picture of how people actually dress in your future job environment.

Your first interviews with people in your profession are excellent sources of information about business clothes and many other subjects. There is no substitute for personal observation. All you need to do at the beginning of your market campaign is to combine a conservative approach toward dress with the realization that a good fit, and colors that you enjoy wearing, help you make a favorable impression. Extremes of any kind only get in the way of establishing rapport with interviewers.

Rely on demonstrating your uniqueness by your attitude and abilities, not by being in the forefront of fashionable dress. At the same time, pay your interviewers the compliment of caring how you appear on an interview.

Dress will not be the major factor in successful interviewing and obtaining job offers. But it can diminish your chances if it is extreme or careless. The best way to be sure about your appearance is to observe successful people in your field. And the best opportunity for this occurs at the time of your interviews.

When you start going on interviews, you will need to set up a record-keeping system. There are two great advantages in keeping an accurate record of all your market campaign activities. First, it enables you to see progress and success. Second, it makes your follow-through steps more effective. Timing is an important factor in sending follow-up letters and making telephone calls. From a number of possible record-keeping systems, I will describe the one that has been used with the greatest success by our clients.

Every time you start to approach a person, write his or her name on a blank sheet of paper. Add the address and phone number, as well as any information you have about the person. Use telegram-style phrases, so you can scan it easily later. As your relationship proceeds, you will be adding more information about the person. Write the date and a brief description of every contact you have with this contact on the sheet. List all letters (date and type of letters), phone calls, and interviews. Attach copies of all correspondence to this sheet. Keep all such contact sheets in alphabetical order. Your contact sheets will be a valuable resource not only during your market campaign but throughout your career.

Example

James S. Miller, Marketing Mgr.
Ritz Mfg. Corp., 653 7th Ave.
New York, N.Y., Tel: 212-453-4500
(Referred by: John Perkins, Sales Mgr., American Global Corp.)

Description: Late forties, tall, thinks all salesmen should be tall; brisk; doesn't like wasting time.

Letter	1/5/79	(copy attached)
T.C.	1/11/79	left message
T.C.	1/12/79	out of town—to return 1/13 late
T.C.	1/14/79	set appointment for 1/20/79 11:30 A.M.
Interview	1/20/79	(35 minutes) J. M. said this was more time than he usually gave people (green light?), liked resume, asked many questions about my computer experience. Suggested I talk with Ernest Gluck, V.P. Marketing at Bromfield Mfg. Co. and Madeleine Summers, word processing specialist at Argo Engineering.
		Wants to see me again after I have seen the two people above. Told him I would call to set appointment next week.
T-Y letter	1/20/79	(copy attached)

If you are not already using an appointment calendar, buy a small one that you can carry in your pocket or handbag. It serves the dual purpose of helping you be organized and making you look organized.

As described in Chapter 6, Referral interviews are going to take up at least two-thirds of the time you devote to your total market campaign. Remember, this approach opens the door to the best job opportunities with the highest income potential. These are the jobs that never reach the public through formal channels of employment. They are usually filled as soon as they become vacant, and many are created to fit special needs in an organization. They are publicized through word of mouth, if at all.

The remaining one-third of job opportunities are published, advertised, or handled by job brokers. By comparison with the "informal" two-thirds of the job market, they are lower in quality, but in numbers they are still considerable. If you have solid, continuous experience and well-defined skills, such as engineering, sales, or secretarial, you will do well in this sector of the market. If you are more specialized or wish to change careers, put more of your efforts into the informal or Referral approach to the market. If you are looking for a senior-level or management position, the "formal" part of the market amounts to no more than a small percentage of the total job market. Most of the information about opportunities will come to you through your contacts.

Whatever your level, the "formal" job market should never be ignored, because effective approaches to that market can be made with a minimum expenditure of time and energy. Here are some guidelines:

Select the newspaper in your city or region that carries the largest number of classified ads. The trend across the country is away from the "Help Wanted" ads to "Career Opportunities." For higher-level positions, also get a newspaper that carries national advertising, such as *The New York Times* or *The Wall Street Journal*. Also discover, through library and word-of-mouth research, which professional or trade publications carry job and career advertisements in your field. For instance, many universities and government agencies publish their own job listings. In most cases, these are not widely publicized, which means that the positions listed in them do not generate as much competition as those receiving wider circulation.

Because Sunday papers carry the most ads, plan to spend a part of every Sunday answering two or three ads (midweek for *The Wall Street Journal*). Competition is heavy for these jobs, so it is essential to respond to ads as soon as possible after their publication. Some of the positions advertised will be filled by the time they come to your attention. Some are advertised only to meet a legal requirement; they are often actually filled even before they are advertised. And a number of individual job ads are inserted by employment agencies and recruiting firms, but there is frequently no way of identifying them.

Keep in mind, however, that up to 20 percent of all job offers are actually made to people who originally responded to an advertisement, and take an efficient approach to this sector of the job market. That way you can maximize your results while minimizing time and effort expended.

In answering job opportunity ads, follow these rules:

First answer "company" ads that clearly identify the sponsoring organization. Such ads give you the greatest chance for a competitive edge. They enable you to identify and directly approach decision-makers in these organizations, using techniques you have learned and practiced as well as avoiding the bottleneck of the personnel departments. Look for job descriptions that are compatible with your Success Factors, even though the qualifications asked for may not entirely match yours. These ads are a good way of making contact with individuals and their organizations. Once you have made personal contact, you have an excellent chance of controlling the interviews and relating your talents and skills to the needs of the organization.

Place yourself in the strongest possible position for obtaining an interview by using a dual approach in responding to this kind of ad.

Because any good ad published in the mass media draws a

vast number of responses, there is no way for the recipient of
these responses to evaluate them or even read them carefully.
A quick scan is all you can reasonably expect. For this reason,
make it possible for the reader to get vital information in the
few seconds he or she is able to give your response. The question "Is this response relevant to the job we are trying to fill?"
must be answered clearly and quickly. You can achieve this
dramatically by using the "quick-response letter" described in
Chapter 7.

The second step of the dual response to a "company" ad is
a letter to a senior executive of the organization that placed
the ad. This should take the shape of a standard letter of approach, described in Chapter 7. The easiest way to identify
the executive to whom you will write is to call the company
switchboard and ask for the name of the person in charge of
the area in which you expect to work. Names of such senior
executives can also be found in industrial directories available
at libraries, but these directories are partially out of date by
the time they are published; so verify any information they
contain by a telephone call to the company before you write.

In very small organizations, the president or director makes
all hiring decisions, and a letter asking for an interview should
be addressed to him or her.

As I pointed out in other chapters, no such letter should be
written as an application for a specific job, because this would
put the recipient under pressure to make a commitment to
consider you for such a job in advance of the interview. Also,
the advertised job may be filled by that time. The immediate
reason for writing this letter is that the organization has identified itself as having needs in your area of interest. The larger
purpose of writing to a specific person is your intention to add
him or her to your contact network. You know that there is a
mutual interest, and, even if there is no immediate opportunity, there may be one in the future.

The ad should *not* be mentioned in this letter of approach because it might trigger an automatic mechanism by which your letter will be included in the large stack of responses to the original ad and might never reach the person to whom you are writing.

There have been occasions where both of these responses to an ad have ended up on the desk of the same person. There is nothing wrong with this. It is usually seen as a sign of effectiveness and strong interest in the organization on the applicant's part. While this approach does not make answering help wanted ads an ideal job-finding method, it will significantly increase your success rate in the "formal" sector of the job market.

The second type of ad, the blind ad, needs a different response. There is no way to use a personal follow-through method because you will not, in most cases, be able to identify the organization involved. The most effective way to reply to a blind ad is a quick-response letter.

Over the years our clients have documented that the first letter of response to an ad is frequently overlooked due to the large volume of answers received. For this reason, send a duplicate response two or three days later. A carbon copy or photocopy may be used for this. If the first rush of responses does not produce enough qualified applicants, the following day's mail is usually looked at more carefully.

Treat the answering of blind ads as a routine activity. Because the quality level of the positions offered is generally low, compared with word-of-mouth job opportunities, and the yield is equally low, a volume approach is the only realistic one. Yet, enough job offers are made every week to people answering such ads to warrant continuous attention to this area.

To summarize: The answering of job ads can be seen as a way to make contact. Once you are sitting face to face with an interviewer, you can take a measure of control. And you can put into practice the interview and negotiating techniques you have learned.

A different strategy is required in dealing with employment agencies, recruiting firms, and other job brokers.

Once you have focused your job and career objective, keep your eyes and ears open for reputable and effective agencies in your career area. While it is a sign of ethical practices for an agency to belong to a local, state, or national professional organization and to be licensed, it is not always a sign of effectiveness. The best information, as usual, comes from people who have successfully used job brokers. Both individuals who found a good job and employers who found good individuals are in a position to recommend good agencies.

Select three agencies about which you have better-than-average information and contact them. Use a letter of approach and a follow-up telephone call to make an appointment with a person in each agency. This is normally done only by senior-level professionals, but there is every reason for you to look and act like a professional, whatever your level. You will be taken more seriously and treated with more respect, and your results will be better than average.

The selection of appropriate agencies depends on your career field. Although the majority of agencies prefer to be known as generalists, in fact most have developed specialized areas in which they function better than in others. Some agencies specialize in finance and computers. Recruiting and search firms, popularly known as head hunters, focus on senior-level executives.

Even though these firms prefer to take the initiative and search out qualified individuals whom they wish to market, long experience has shown that they often respond to information transmitted to them by a senior-level job seeker.

Therefore, they should be approached like any other job broker.

There are a number of precautions to observe in dealing with agencies of any kind:

The agency benefits most when you accept a position, even though the actual fee is now usually paid by the employer. The employer will make his requirements known to the agency. Later disappointment to everyone involved can be avoided if you also make your requirements known to the agency, including your Success Factors as stated in your job objective.

You will be asked about your salary requirements. Make sure you give a minimum figure that is higher than the average in the field. You may have to do some research to find that figure. In most cases, your minimum figure will become the figure on which any offers are based. If the person with whom you are dealing at the agency objects that your minimum salary requirement is higher than your current or previous income figure, remind him or her that you need help not in manufacturing your career, but in advancing it.

Because of the volume of job seekers at agencies, it is impossible for agencies to keep track of all job seekers. Call each agency you have contacted once a week to remind them of your existence. This will also tell them that you are on an active search and are more likely to do well on your interviews.

Not much needs to be said about the placing of "Position Wanted" ads. Such ads have generally been ineffective in producing job opportunities, although they often attract a large volume of unsolicited junk mail. The only exception is a notice advertising your availability in certain specialized trade publications where the ad cost is very low, or ads may be inserted free of charge. But do not expect much from this approach.

Another fringe approach to job hunting is the mass mailing

of self-marketing letters, also known as confetti letters. The time saved by such mass mailings turns out to be an illusion, when results are considered. Five carefully targeted letters of the types described in this book will generate more serious interviews than five hundred confetti letters. And they cost less and take less time.

How many interviews does it take to get a good job? There is no real answer. There is, of course, a statistical mean, but it would be dangerous to gear your expectations to such a figure as a guideline. Experience shows that people who take longer than they expected to find the right job are often tempted to accept an inferior job offer.

The average number of interviews is an irrelevant consideration. The correct number is the one that produces the right job for you. The only way to reduce the number of interviews is to increase the quality of each interview. You can do this if you keep yourself mentally and physically in good condition, by balancing time spent on a concentrated market campaign with time spent on restoring your energy during leisure time, and by constantly showing interest in other people as expressed during interviews and in thank-you letters.

Getting an offer on the first, second, or third interview is often considered "lucky." In reality, however, it may not always be a good thing. Your interviews provide you with information. This information becomes the data base from which you make your job and career decisions. The interviews also help you generate your contact network. Everyone needs to build and maintain a contact network to assure constant career advancement. Our experience shows that ten to twelve Referral interviews are required to build any kind of useful data base and to get a feel for career advancement options. Many people have built a momentum that carried them to great heights in their careers following a market campaign that consisted of forty or more interviews. It may not sound reasonable to go on forty interviews just to get a job, and it isn't. But forty interviews to get a career started that never stops moving—that's a good return on investment!

The key to a successful market campaign is activity. If you fill your market campaign with planned, purposeful activity, everyone you come in contact with will see you as a productive and successful person.

By now it should be clear that there is enough opportunity for purposeful activity for an eight-hour-a-day market campaign if you are unemployed. Two interviews a day, answering ads, always writing new letters of approach, visiting and telephoning agencies, doing library research, making follow-up calls, and, *always*, writing thank-you letters—this is a total market campaign.

A note about the production of letters: Because quality takes precedence over quantity, there is not enough typing involved to warrant hiring a professional typist. Most of our clients find that even using only two fingers, they can type all their own letters. You can usually borrow a typewriter if you don't own one. If finances allow, you may want to buy or rent one. It's a good thing to have. You may also be successful in getting members of your family or friends to volunteer for help in typing letters.

Speaking of finances, you may discover that it takes more time to generate the right job offers than you anticipated, and your financial resources are being depleted at a rapid rate. You should consider a Stop-Loss Job. You can then continue your market campaign from a position of greater financial security, while, of course, doing a good job for your employer. During periods of economic recession, stories are frequently published about Ph.D.s pumping gas. There is nothing demeaning about a carefully planned, purposeful step, designed to support an active market campaign.

One of the most important things to remember during your

market campaign, and throughout your career, is that there is always a Next Step. Sometimes it may be difficult to determine what you should do next, but you can always be sure there is a logical Next Step!

Sometimes contact with a person or an organization seems to have produced a dead end. In such a case the Next Step may not be taken until months or even years later; but the potential is always there. The ubiquitous thank-you letter is a good example of this; it is a Next Step in itself, and it will generate the Next Step by its effect on the recipient. It should bring about a positive feeling in the reader, encouraging him or her to talk about you to others, or to consider you for a future position. It may generate a second interview. The thank-you letter may contain a request for information that will be provided; and in some cases thank-you letters motivate people to write thank-you letters for the thank-you letters they receive.

To summarize: If you can't think of the Next Step at any point in your market campaign, review the appropriate chapter. There is always a Next Step.

9
The
Job Interview

The high point of every market campaign is the job interview. This is where the time and effort you spent on preparation, research, contact building, and Referral interviews is producing tangible results. Let's put the job interview in perspective.

The structure of job finding is simple. There are only two types of interviews: the Referral interview and the job interview.

Any interview during which a *specific job opportunity* is discussed is a job interview. Any other interview is, by definition, a Referral interview. Even if possible *future* job opportunities are considered, you are still on a Referral interview. Only when the interviewer says in so many words that you are being considered for a specific job, or for employment at this time, are you on a job interview.

If you are in doubt about the purpose of an interview, ask the interviewer to enlighten you. Questions like "Are we talking about a specific job possibility?" or "Are you considering me for a specific position?" will help you establish the purpose of your discussion and allow you to accomplish that purpose. Many interviewers have difficulty structuring an interview; your questions will help both you and the interviewer to become aware of the actual purpose and goal of an interview and increase the likelihood of success.

137

Sometimes a Referral interview can turn into a job interview. In such a case it is doubly important that this shift in purpose is clearly understood by both you and the interviewer.

There are two ground rules for job interviews. You must:

1. Deal with the objectives and needs of both you and your interviewer; not one or the other, but both.
2. Retain control over the interview.

For many people, the job interview turns out to be a trap. The applicant's purpose is to get the job which meets his or her requirements, while the potential employer's purpose is to find a solution to his or her own problem. Both participants in the interview are centered on themselves and their own problems. They are separated by a desk and several miles of divergent interests. It is your job to close the gap during the interview.

Most job seekers turn control of a job interview over to the interviewer at the beginning of the meeting. This is unfair as well as unproductive. No interviewer can be fully aware of your purposes and goals, and no interview can produce useful results unless the goals of both participants are considered and met.

What should your purpose be at the first interview for a job? To get the job? Certainly not! To get a job offer? Equally unrealistic. Offers of jobs worth having are rarely made during the first interview.

The only real purpose of a first interview for a job is to get the second interview.

Despite the seemingly limited purpose of the first interview, its importance is crucial. It gives you an opportunity to find the interviewer's wavelength, to establish rapport on the human level. If this purpose is accomplished, all subsequent interviews may be mere formalities, and with good follow-through the job offer is virtually assured.

As in the Referral interview, establishing rapport during a job interview is not always easy. However, if you free yourself from the pressure of having to make the sale on this first interview, you will find it much easier to concentrate on the real purpose to be accomplished.

Sometimes your first interview for a job takes place with a middleman: a recruiter or personnel officer. In that case, your objective will be to get to the person for whom you will be working when you are in the job. The ground rules for such a first job interview are the same. Your purpose is to establish rapport with the interviewer in order to be invited for the next interview.

Here are the guidelines for a successful first job interview:

- Arrive on time. This means arrive early! Besides ensuring against unforeseen delays, it gives you an opportunity to become more aware of the people and the physical conditions in which you will be interviewing and perhaps working. It is very difficult to overcome the negative impression of arriving late for an interview, whatever the reason.
- Dress well but on the conservative side. It is not possible to make a mistake by doing this. Your uniqueness will be established by your attitude and your well-prepared presentation, not by your clothes.
- Make this a listening interview. Show genuine interest in your interviewer. This interest cannot be manufactured. While you are focused solely on your own problem, such as the need to become employed and to produce an income, you can never feel or show a real interest in the other person.

Remember, you will never convince a future employer of your relevance to his organization unless you are able to relate your abilities and experience to his needs. In order to do this effectively, you need to know and understand those needs. This task is complicated by the fact that many interviewers themselves have an inadequate understanding of their own needs and frequently are not able to verbalize them.

This gives you an opportunity to perform a genuine service for your interviewer. By asking intelligent questions (not stereotyped or prefabricated ones) you will help the interviewer define his needs and purposes with regard to the job for which you are being interviewed.

There are people who have trained themselves to be in a listening mode, but not to actually hear what is being said. It is essential to hear what your interviewer says and to demonstrate that you have heard by your expression as well as by your response and the questions you ask.

The purpose of asking questions should be to gain greater understanding. Responses should indicate that you have understood. Resist the temptation to suggest solutions to the interviewer's problems. It is easy to offend an interviewer by producing answers, right or wrong, in five minutes to problems with which the interviewer has struggled for five years. However, suggest to the interviewer that your experience makes you a likely person to help him or her solve such problems when you are in the job. It is even better to give one or more examples of past achievements that demonstrate your problem-solving ability.

Our client, Richard S., was asked during a job interview how he would go about reducing employee turnover in the interviewer's organization. Richard knew the company had been saddled with this problem for years. He avoided the dual risks of offending his interviewer by either questioning the organization's fairness to its employees or dealing with a complex problem on the spot. Richard said: "I don't know enough about your company to come up with any immediate solutions, but I'd like to tell you about the approaches I've used in the past to solve turnover problems." He then gave two examples from his past experience, where his actions resulted in re-

ducing employee turnover. Because he had reviewed his experience and accomplishments in preparation for his market
campaign, he sounded and looked confident about his abilities.

The interviewer liked Richard's attitude and self-confidence, even though he wasn't sure his situation was similar to
the examples Richard related. The interviewer decided to
take a chance and made a job offer.

Richard is certain that any concrete solution to the interviewer's immediate problem would have been rejected as either not being applicable or as having already been tried!
There was also the unlikely chance that Richard would have
accidentally hit on the right solution. Then the interviewer
might have tried to implement the solution without Richard,
which would very likely have been detrimental to both of
them.

At this point it is necessary to understand the process of
making hiring decisions.

All hiring decisions are based on emotions first, on judgments regarding your technical qualifications second. Simply
put, that means "If I like you, I may hire you. If I don't, I
won't."

There is overwhelming evidence that hiring decisions heavily based on emotions are frequently very successful. Realizing and accepting this fact of life will make it infinitely easier
to get job offers. Your primary objective on your first job interview, as well as subsequent ones, is to make a favorable impression. The best way to accomplish this is to care, and show
you care, about the person who sits across the desk from you.
This, in turn, is best done by putting your own job desires and
requirements on the shelf during the first stages of the job interview process. Once a job offer has been made to you, there
is ample time to make sure that your own needs are dealt
with.

The above does not imply that you don't need to be technically qualified for the job for which you are being interviewed, only that such qualifications are a secondary consideration. Gaps in your qualifications can be overcome, but poor rapport with your interviewer is much more difficult to deal with. There are exceptions, of course. If your name is Einstein and you have developed a theory of relativity, you will probably be considered for a position on your technical qualifications alone.

During the first stages of a job interview, the average interviewer will invite you to talk about yourself. The phrase "Tell me about yourself!" not only signifies a request for information but is also an attempt to get the interview moving. Your response can, and usually will, establish the course of at least part of the interview. This great opportunity can be a dangerous, if unconsciously set, trap.

If you are not prepared for the question, you are as likely to talk yourself out of a job as into it. At that point in the interview, you will have little information about the interviewer's needs, problems, expectations, and prejudices. You will be moving in a minefield of wrong emphases, negative information, and, at best, irrelevant facts. You can turn this request into an opportunity by, in turn, asking the interviewer which parts of your background he or she is most interested in or would like you to talk about first.

Any interviewer who has had experience with long-winded, autobiographical narratives will welcome the opportunity to help you make your response relevant. If the choice is left to you, and you have few clues to the interviewer's specific interests, you can never go wrong by talking about areas of strength, your achievements. If you have done your homework, you can describe your work history entirely in terms of accomplishments, results, and success. Make it brief and be sure, every now and then, that your interviewer is still listening with interest. Rather than going on too long, ask, "Would you like me to go into more detail?" or "Would you like me to talk more about . . . ?"

Leave out failures and weaknesses. They are not helpful to your future employer. Even when motivated by modesty, references to failures serve only to set up roadblocks in the interviewer's mind. A good example of this is the fact, noted earlier, that many people apologize for their resumes to their interviewers. The reason for such apologies is sometimes modesty on the part of the job seeker who feels uncomfortable about giving the impression of bragging about his or her record of accomplishments. Otherwise it is the realization that a career cannot be adequately described on one or two pieces of paper. Whatever the reason, the unspoken reaction on the part of the interviewer is always negative: Either you were unwilling to put more effort into writing a good resume, or worse, you were unable to. The usefulness of the resume has now been effectively destroyed.

Substituting strengths for weaknesses is also an important factor in answering sensitive questions during a job interview. There are questions that probe for possible obstacles to your being considered for a job, as well as hidden weaknesses that might create future problems. Understand the purpose underlying such questions and you will answer them successfully.

Probing questions are asked to gain reassurance, not to gather data. It's that simple!

Every hiring decision involves risk. The interviewer's aim is to reduce this risk as much as possible. The factual information contained in your answers is far less useful than the attitude behind the information. There are some areas in which it is difficult for any interviewer to get factual information. One of these is the area of human relations. Will you fit into the organization? Will you work well with others? Can you accept leadership? Can you provide leadership?

Another area about which interviewers need as much reassurance as they can get is your level of motivation. Granted that you *can* do the job, *will* you do it?

Some of the questions you may be asked may seem quite personal. Some interviewers use so-called stress techniques to test your behavior under pressure. The extreme type of stress interview, during which a candidate is deliberately insulted in order to test his responses, has fortunately gone out of fashion, but a mild form of it is still used by many interviewers.

An excellent way to answer all probing questions is to make brief and positive statements. This is not as easy as it sounds. But you can create a favorable impression by taking a few seconds to reflect on each question and make a brief positive statement that shows you have no problem in the area the question seeks to explore.

Here are some typical questions frequently asked our clients during job interviews, as well as the answers that have proven most effective.

Q: How did you like your last job?
A: I learned a lot; it was an important part of my career. (Note: Never say anything negative about a former job or employer. Your interviewer will see you as a complainer.)

Q: How did you get along with your former boss?
A: I have always (usually) had a good relationship with my employer.

Q: If you had to live the last ten years of your life over again, what would you do differently?
A: I feel good about the decisions I've made during the last ten years. I don't think I would change very much. Alternate answer: I feel very fortunate about what happened to me during the last ten years. (We all like to hire lucky/successful people!)

Q: Did you ever make any suggestions to management in a former job?

A: Yes. (Describe a specific suggestion that was accepted by and benefited a former employer.)

Q: Tell me about the greatest disappointment in your life.

A: Everyone has disappointments. I don't usually have a problem dealing with them. (You might give an example where you have overcome the effects of an adverse event. Remember, the interviewer does not care about the actual event but wants to know how you deal with adversity.)

Q: What are some of your weaknesses? (Danger! Bite your tongue and say:)

A: I can't think of any that would affect my work. (Note: Although this is a frequent question, it is not a reasonable one, because it invites you to incriminate yourself. Answering it as if it were a reasonable question has eliminated many candidates from the running.)

Q: What do you think your employers could have done to help you function better as an employee? (Another sandtrap! This is a test of your willingness to take initiative and responsibility rather than letting your employers make decisions for you and then blaming them for your failures.)

A: I feel my employers have always been supportive. I do not have a problem with this.

Q: If you could have the choice of any job, what would you do?

A: I would choose a job in which I could use my abilities and experience in . . . (give two or three strong areas).

Q: What does your spouse think about the kind of work you do?

A: I have always had his/her full support.

Q: Assuming we make you an offer, what do you see as your future?

A: I would first do the job you are offering me to the best of my ability. Eventually I would hope to earn a chance for advancement by increasing my contributions to the organization. (Most people skip over the job for which they are considered and talk about advancement only, thereby telling the interviewer that this job is an insignificant stepping stone to the next job, a major turn-off to employers.)

Some job interview questions attempt to explore specific problem areas. If you expect to be asked any of the questions listed below, you should formulate answers in advance, so you can be well prepared and self-confident during the interview.

Q: Doesn't this job represent a career switch for you?

A: Not really. I'll be using the same abilities and skills. (Give examples of your abilities that form a connecting link between your past jobs and the one for which you are being interviewed.)

Q: (If you have no academic degree): But you don't have a degree! (This sounds like a statement, but it's really a question, or rather a request for reassurance. If lack of a degree disqualified you, you wouldn't be in the room.)

A: I feel I have the equivalent of a degree in terms of training, ability, and experience.

Q: Aren't you overqualified for this job?

A: It would allow me to use some of my greatest abilities, and I feel I could bring something new to the job that the average applicant might not be able to. (Or, if it is true): The job environment is more important to me than the specific job description. If I did my job well, I feel there would be an opportunity to advance in this organization.

Q: (If you are a woman): Do you plan to have children? (Remember, the employer is interested only in exploring possible future problem areas; he has no other interest in the subject.)

A: I have considered this, and discussed it with my husband. It will not interfere with my career. (Make sure this statement is based on fact; you may be asked to give details, such as the

length of time for which you expect to be absent from your job.)
An alternate and quite satisfactory answer may be: I have no
such plans for the foreseeable future.

Q: Aren't you a little young (old) for this job?
A: I feel my age gives me certain advantages. (Specify: old—experience, judgment; young—high energy level, ability to learn.)

Q: Why did you leave your last job? (If you have been fired, and
the interviewer knows it.)
A: I had a personality conflict with my superior; you know how
hard it sometimes is to overcome such things.
(Note: This is one instance where mention of a personality/in-
compatibility problem is permissible. It is almost always a factor in a termination and, because most people have had such an
experience, they will generally accept this answer. Avoid a detailed defense of your part in the event. It serves no purpose;
instead move on to a more positive subject. If you were terminated because of an organizational change or any other reason
beyond your control, then, of course, there is a problem. But
even then it is advisable to be brief in your explanation and
move on.)

Q: Have you ever had a nervous breakdown? (If you have had
one.)
A: Yes, but that was some time ago, and I haven't had any problem in years. (You might add): In fact, the experience taught me
how to deal with stress situations much better.

All of us have gaps in our arsenal of qualifications. You will
probably never be interviewed for a job for which you are 100
percent qualified. What is important is that you learn how to
fill the gaps during an interview, how to substitute positive information for negative information. You can make a habit of
responding to: "But you don't have. . ." with: "That's true, but
I do have. . ."

Interestingly, once you are prepared to give such positive answers, you will usually not even need them! Your interviewers will not perceive a problem, and they won't need to seek reassurance in those areas.

I had a client who had had what is popularly known as a nervous breakdown. When he told me of his many unsuccessful job interviews, he said, "I knew I was lost every time they asked me about my nervous breakdown." I asked, "How did they know about your breakdown?" "I don't know," he said. What had really happened was that he looked so shaky on his interviews that people jumped to one of the two most obvious conclusions: a drinking problem or a nervous breakdown.

We discussed the issue, and it developed that my client had had no problem for the past five years. Once he learned to substitute positive information for his "problem," he soon got a job offer. When he called to tell me about his interview, I asked him, "But what about your breakdown?" He said, "I forgot all about it, and they never asked."

Other sensitive questions may concern lack of academic certification, experience in a field that may be only tenuously related to the interviewer's field, and a long period of unemployment. An interviewer can, and frequently will, override these problems when you make a favorable impression. But when you are convinced that these problems are genuine obstacles to getting an offer, you will communicate this conviction to your interviewer.

Our records show that physical handicaps, including total blindness, are far easier to deal with than many real or imaginary mental problems. Constantly focus the interviewer's attention on the real issue—your ability to do the job.

One of the major obstacles in the interview process is stereotyping. This is true whether the stereotyping is done by the interviewer or the interviewee. To assume that every interviewer is guilty of discriminatory practices, until proven innocent, is just as destructive as assuming, for example, that all business is dehumanizing or that all women hate working for other women. You have the right to be treated as a unique individual by an interviewer. You also have an obligation to treat your interviewer the same way.

Before you leave the first interview for a job, make sure you have enough information about your interviewer's problems, needs, and expectations to make an intelligent presentation on the second interview. That way, you will be able to relate your abilities to those problems, needs, and expectations.

You may not always be able to get a good job description, because few employers have a clear idea of how a job is structured, theirs or anyone else's. But you can usually get your interviewer to talk about his or her expectations with regard to the ideal candidate for the job. A direct question ("What are some of the qualifications you would expect the right candidate for this job to have?") is the best way to get information.

Sometimes the interviewer may not have given the job description enough thought, and you may need to probe and ask for amplification and clarification. This is an entirely positive and productive activity, because it benefits both you and the interviewer. And it gives you information on which to base your follow-through with the interviewer. It enables you to stay on his or her wavelength.

Whenever possible, try to set up a date for the second interview. Tell the interviewer you enjoyed the interview, found it productive, and are looking forward to the second meeting.

Then go home and write a thank-you letter. Write it before the end of the same day, while the interview is fresh in your mind.

Refer to the highlights of the interview in the letter to demonstrate that you were listening and your interest was and is high. Pick out one or two points made by the interviewer during the description of his requirements and give a few examples to show that your experience is relevant. Most of the job of relating your abilities to the interviewer's needs should be left for the next face-to-face interview. Declare your intention to deal with unclear or negative issues (if any) at your next meeting. Don't discuss them in the letter. The thank-you letter should reflect enthusiasm. It should also be brief, like all business letters. It should end by describing the Next Step, usually the date of your next meeting. If no date for the next meeting has been set, end the thank-you letter by saying that you will call in a few days to set a day for the next meeting.

Many clients have told us that their thank-you letters were the single, most identifiable factor in getting a job offer in a competitive market.

During the second interview, and any subsequent ones, your purpose will be to fit yourself into your interviewer's frame of reference, insofar as it is compatible with your own career objectives. The rapport you have established during the first meeting will make it easier for you to accomplish this.

After the first interview, your goal will be to receive a job offer. Depending on the nature of the job for which you are being considered, it may take two, three, or more interviews before an offer is made.

Until you get a job offer, talk only about what you can do for the interviewer. After the offer has been made, you will talk about what the interviewer can do for you. This means that salary negotiations should *never* take place before a job offer is made. Yet, you will be asked about your earning expectations, as well as your past earnings. It is essential that you avoid mention of any specific figures at this time. Giving a figure, past or future, will limit your ability to negotiate later.

Until the interviewer is ready to offer you the job, he makes no commitment to you. You are, therefore, not negotiating from a position of strength. The next chapter will show how you can successfully negotiate salary as well as other compensation and benefits.

Until you have reason to believe that the interviewer is satisfied with your ability to do the job, all references to income levels or figures should be turned aside politely with a statement like this: "I'd like to postpone salary discussions until I fully understand the nature of the job we are talking about." Or: "Salary isn't the most important thing to me. If the job is right for me, I'm prepared to be quite flexible with regard to salary." (Of course you will be flexible, but within reason!)

Another response to premature salary questions is "Once you have decided that I'm right for the job, I will be glad to talk about salary. I'm sure your income structure is a fair one, and I will have no problem fitting in."

It is essential to be firm on this. Among our thousands of clients, only a handful have lost job opportunities by withholding a salary figure and, mostly, these were not opportunities worth having. Anyone who is genuinely interested in considering you for employment will not be put off by your firmness of purpose regarding salary discussions.

But many qualified people *are* losing job opportunities and earnings every day by giving away information about salary levels and expectations that do not match those of their interviewers. At best they are losing substantial amounts of income by making later negotiations difficult. Once a figure has been mentioned, it usually stands as a maximum.

If I were to question you about your income requirements and you asked for $20,000, I would probably make a mental note to offer you $18,000 to start with, although I might have been willing to go as high as $27,000—if I thought you were the right person for the job. As a matter of fact, I might never make you the offer. I might feel that a $20,000 person couldn't do a $27,000 job. Of course, I might be wrong, but that would be cold comfort to you. More about this in the following chapter.

One more thing: Resist the urge to evaluate or reject the job before it is offered. By being negative too early, you may give away an opportunity for negotiating a mediocre offer into a good one. And anyway, there is always time to turn it down later.

In the following chapter, you will learn how to conclude the job interviewing process by negotiating the highest possible price for your services.

10 Negotiating The Job Offer

How valuable are you to an employer? What is a "good" salary offer?

The answers to these questions depend on three factors. First, how confident are you of your value, and how well can you communicate this to others? Second, how much are you worth to your prospective employer, given his needs, problems, and the income range and structure in his organization? And third, how good are you at negotiating a sizable increase over an initial salary offer?

Why is it necessary to *negotiate* a job offer?

Because most of us are conditioned to accept what we are offered. However, interviewers rarely offer the maximum compensation at the beginning. This is natural. Every competent business person will want to buy a product or a person's services at the lowest reasonable price. It is up to you to demonstrate that you have something of value to offer and to put the highest reasonable price on your services.

Prepare the ground for this phase of the interview by relating your strengths in terms of ability and experience to the interviewer's requirements, and it will be easier to negotiate a good price. The interviewer will be influenced by your judgment of your value. Your task is to convince him or her that

153

you are exactly right for the job and that the job is exactly right for you.

The three rules for this are simple. First, find out what your interviewer needs and wants by listening and asking questions. Second, talk about *only* those of your abilities, experiences, and past accomplishments that relate directly to the interviewer's stated needs. And third, make a straightforward statement that you can do the job because your abilities match the organization's needs.

In order to make this statement, you must, of course, believe it to be true. There is no need to accomplish the above in one interview. You can do a better job if you spread it over two or three interviews. This strategy gives you time to plan your responses between interviews, and the interviewer will get used to seeing you as the right choice for the position.

If you are not sure that you have convinced the interviewer, ask the question "Do you agree that I am right for the job?" Until that has been established, all questions of money should be turned aside using the approach described in the last chapter. Keep asking specific questions to get a good picture of the job requirements and make sure that you show your understanding of the job, your ability to do it, and your enthusiasm for it.

At the point where you and the interviewer agree on your suitability for the job, it becomes relevant to talk about money—not before. And remember, without an offer of money, there is no job offer.

Whenever possible, wait for your interviewer to bring up the subject of your compensation. Any potential employer who talks to you about compensation at this point signifies he has decided that you are right for the job. This commitment puts you in a favorable negotiating position.

Remember this throughout the negotiating phase: The interviewer has made a mental commitment to you. He or she is on *your* side. That doesn't mean the interviewer will give

NEGOTIATING THE JOB OFFER

away money, but the inclination is to accommodate you as far as possible.

There are specific negotiating techniques that you can use to encourage an interviewer's inclination to accommodate you. Interviewers generally don't start the discussion of compensation with an offer of a specific salary figure. Usually this discussion starts with one or more questions about your past income, your salary requirements, your basic income needs or expectations. All these questions can be summarized in one question: How much will it take to make you accept the offer?

What should your response be to all these questions?

Your unspoken aim will be to get the highest possible offer. There is no way for you to know how far the employer can stretch, given sufficient motivation to do so. Any research you may have done on the organization will give you only their overall salary structure. But almost every range for any specific position can be expanded, given a person with unique qualifications and enthusiasm for the job. You will have had the opportunity to demonstrate your unique qualifications and your high level of motivation during the earlier stages of the job interview.

An interviewer always has a starting salary figure in mind, as well as a range within which he or she can move to improve the offer, if necessary. Your first aim is to discover that starting figure.

If *you* mention a figure, you will have erected a roadblock beyond which you can go only with great difficulty. What is worse, the interviewer may perceive your figure as your maximum salary hope and is likely to offer a lower figure.

As you know, your assessment of your worth may even have a negative effect if it is too far out of range of the prospective employer's thinking. Whether it is too high or too low, it will usually make any further negotiations impossible.

Your best response to all salary questions is to ask what figure the interviewer had in mind. You might say, "It would be presumptuous of me to tell you what the job is worth. I'm sure you had a figure in mind. What did you have in mind?" Or: "What is the salary range for this job?" If you are talking about a newly created position, you might ask for the salary level of employees with similar duties.

If any interviewer insists on knowing your previous salary, say that your previous salary was based on a different set of circumstances, and you would only be giving misleading information. In any case, you would prefer to fit into the organization's current salary structure. Sometimes you can give a future-oriented salary figure, such as this: "The job you have described, if carried out in a superior manner, should be worth about $30,000 in three or four years." Most interviewers will agree to your figure or one in that general range. The reason for this is that three or four years are a long way off, and no interviewer will mind promising you a high future salary, assuming that you will be doing a superior job.

After you have received the interviewer's agreement, say, "Since we agree that the job will be worth $30,000 in three or four years, I'm content to leave the starting salary up to you. What do you think would be a reasonable figure?"

By demonstrating your high expectations, both in job performance and income, you have raised the interviewer's sights and motivated him or her to offer a reasonable starting figure.

Salary negotiations require tact as well as firmness. None of the questions asked by an interviewer are ever irrelevant to him or her. But that doesn't mean you have to give up control over your side of the negotiations. Accept all questions as reasonable but answer them from *your* point of view.

A typical question is "How much do you need to live on?" It seems like a reasonable question, but a literal answer would not be in your best interest because you want to be paid according to your worth, not your needs. So a good answer would be "I can be quite flexible if I have to be. Money isn't my highest priority. But I feel I have quite a lot to offer to an organization like yours. I'd like my salary to be based on my value *to you*. I'm sure you have a fair income structure for this kind of job—how much do you have in mind?"

All of your efforts should be directed toward obtaining a starting figure for your negotiations, based on an assumption of your value to the organization, at your highest level of productivity, not your minimum needs.

Eventually, your interviewer will mention a figure. What should your response be? You know with reasonable certainty that the initial figure doesn't represent the highest possible salary offer. However, it would be almost impossible to say this to the interviewer. And saying it would serve no purpose.

The most effective response to a starting offer is a thoughtful *silence*. By remaining silent, you are signifying two things: You are carefully considering the offer (courtesy demands this), and you are not satisfied with it. You are certainly not accepting it.

Because the interviewer has already made a commitment to you and is in the buying position, at this point he or she will want to make it possible for you to accept the offer. A thoughtful silence is the most powerful tool you have to signal to the interviewer that you expect more. Any words you could use would only dissipate your energy in fruitless argument about the reasonableness of the interviewer's offer.

We have found that in better than half of all negotiating situations where silence has been used, the interviewer will mention a higher figure without further discussion. The interviewer usually says, "I could go to $. . . ." The reason for this is that most interviewers leave themselves room to negotiate, and you have laid the foundation for enlarging the offer by establishing your values to the interviewer in advance of the actual salary negotiations.

In most cases where the offer is not raised without further discussion, you will either receive an explanation for the size of the offer—to which you will listen politely while continuing your thoughtful silence as long as it is necessary—or you will be asked for a reaction. In the latter case, answer by saying that, although you are enthusiastic about the job opportunity, you feel the salary offer is on the modest side. Follow this with another thoughtful silence. Remember the phrase well known to salespeople: Whoever talks first, loses. This also applies to salary negotiations, but only if both parties are highly motivated to reach agreement.

In some cases you may not be able to reach agreement in one session. The interviewer may need someone else's permission to make a better offer, without wanting to inform you of that fact. The easiest way to deal with this is to offer continuing the discussion at another meeting, preferably the following day. Again, demonstrate your enthusiasm for the job and the organization.

This process is frequently misunderstood as playing hard to get. Being hard to get is a purposeless gambit invented by people who have little understanding of human relations. You should always be eager and ready to make a full commitment to the job being offered, but only under the right circumstances and the right price. The right circumstances are the ones that allow you to best use your skills and talents in an environment most conducive to getting results. The right price is the highest one your employer is willing to pay.

Why?

A vast number of employers, interviewed by us over the years, have stated and demonstrated in practice a fundamental principle: Employees who have handled themselves well during their salary negotiations were treated with greater respect and were given more opportunities to advance within their organization.

This is sound psychology. If I offer you more money than I originally intended, I certainly will not go around saying that you made me do it against my will. I will assume that my good judgment persuaded me to extend myself, that I made a good investment. I will then be motivated to back up my good judgment by giving you every opportunity to produce a good return on my investment.

Now let's look at some special negotiating situations:

A number of organizations have more or less fixed compensation ranges for certain or all of their job categories. Civil service is an extreme example. But experience over the years has taught us that statements regarding the nonnegotiability of a salary offer frequently only signify that exceptions are rarely made. Unless you have reliable information that a salary structure is fixed beyond human intervention, assume that it is negotiable. You have absolutely nothing to lose by trying, because your interviewer has already made a commitment to you by offering the job in the first place. And your positive attitude toward your own worth will always generate respect.

An example from our files will illustrate this. A client with a Ph.D. from Harvard University, in negotiating a job offer with a telephone company, was told that the salary range for the type of position he was being offered was fixed. He was even shown a booklet giving the range in black and white. He studied the booklet politely and said he thought this to be a very sound compensation system. Then he asked if they had ever had a person of his background with a Ph.D. from Harvard in that position. They said no. He then suggested that he didn't really fit into any of the printed categories and that he would like to discuss establishing a new category or expanding an existing one. After two more meetings, a special income category was created, and he received a much higher offer.

Again, make sure that you are negotiating from a position of competence and compatibility, not need or greed.

If you have been unemployed for a length of time, you will sometimes find it difficult to do a good job negotiating a salary. It is doubly important in a situation like this to negotiate. A number of employers have a prejudicial attitude toward an unemployed candidate. Unreasonable as it is, sometimes a person out of work feels and is treated as damaged goods. If you have studied and followed the suggestions in this book, you will have dealt with this problem. You can eliminate any residual prejudice on your future employer's part by doing a good job in holding up your end of salary negotiations. If you are confident of your value, you can convince your interviewer.

Althea S. had been out of work for four months before becoming our client. She was forty-three years old and had held senior administrative positions for many years. But her self-confidence was at a record low. After a market campaign of seven weeks, she received her first offer as assistant to the vice-president and manager of administrative services at a salary 23 percent below her past income level. The day after she received the offer, Althea came in to see me.

She began our conversation with "I've never been so insulted." But she continued, "I need the work so I guess I'll take it." I was convinced that accepting the job under these circumstances and with this attitude would lead to another firing sooner or later, and I wasn't sure Althea could sustain another blow to her self-respect. So I proposed a deal: If, after one more week, she hadn't received a substantial increase on her current offer, I would agree to her taking that job, at least on a Stop-Loss basis. She felt that after almost six months of unemployment, she could wait one more week and agreed.

We then went to work and analyzed her first interviews with this organization. It turned out that between 60 and 70 percent of the conversations with her interviewer had dealt with the circumstances of her previous termination. The interviews were far from positive. She felt attacked and belittled. It was a tribute to her inherent strength and employment value to be made an offer at all, under the circumstances.

Althea, with my help, assembled what information she had about her future employer's requirements. The picture was incomplete, and she asked for another meeting to clarify her understanding of the job. She asked many questions, which the vice-president answered in great detail, because he needed assistance and had been dwelling on his own problems for some time. Althea and I had more than enough information for planning her strategy for the fourth and final interview. No mention was made at either the third or fourth interviews of her past termination. The subject had been made irrelevant by her positive purpose.

During the fourth interview, she suggested to her interviewer that her new understanding of the scope of the job and the contributions she could make to it made it reasonable to reopen the salary discussion. The interviewer agreed because he now saw Althea as a solution to his problem. As a result she received a new offer 8 percent above, rather than 23 percent below, her former income level, and the title of associate manager of administrative services, instead of assistant to the vice-president and manager of administrative services.

Negotiating skill is based on nothing more mysterious than building a solid data base, convincing the prospective employer of your value, and realizing that negotiating your salary is an acceptable, reasonable, and necessary step in finding a good job.

We have found that women generally have a slight edge in basic negotiating attitudes. Women have not been indoctrinated as heavily as men with traditional assumptions about job finding. Most men, on the other hand, have been told from adolescence that they must accept salary offers as final, and that they always are expected to give a figure in response to a request for one. Another factor is that women are being looked at as special cases by many employers. This is not always a help, but can aid in negotiating special salary offers.

If you are a women, it is essential that you ignore the frequently given advice that you ask for the same salary that is paid to men in the given job. As mentioned above, your value to the organization is the only reasonable criterion for negotiating a good salary offer. Once you ask for consideration on the basis of belonging to a group, you will have given away control over the negotiating process. That isn't to say that you should accept a job under discriminatory conditions with regard to salary or anything else. But you will do better, now and in the future, if you use the opportunity to establish yourself in the employer's mind as a unique, valuable, and self-confident person. Your unique abilities may make you worth *more* than the salary paid to men in a given job!

If you are being pressed for a salary figure, consider the following: Giving a figure is almost certainly going to cost you money, because it limits your ability to negotiate a really good salary offer, beyond the figure you supply. What's more, it means that you are lagging behind every year in the job by the same amount that you lose in your original negotiations. This represents a considerable sum of money over a period of time.

Giving a figure against your best interest is also not a good way to enter into a long-term relationship with your employer. An average salary establishes you as an average person, or worse. High starting salaries generate high salary increases. A person with a comparatively low salary can expect low salary increases.

A common fallacy is that giving a salary range is a way out of this dilemma. If your research has told you that people at your level, in your field, earn from $20,000 to $25,000 annually, it would be a great mistake to tell a prospective employer that you expect your earnings to fall into that range. What you would really be saying is that you would like to make $25,000, but you are willing to accept $20,000. You'd be implying that you see yourself as equal to the lowest earners in your profession, which is not an inspiring image to present to an employer.

At the same time, you can turn a salary range given to you by an interviewer to your advantage. If you are told that a job pays $20,000 to $25,000, pick up the top figure, repeat it back to the interviewer, and say; "That would be a reasonable figure to start from."

If you have exhausted all of your resources to get the interviewer to mention a salary figure, and you are hard pressed to give a figure, past or future, you can give a minimum figure below which you would not go in considering an offer. Make sure you can live with that figure. You may have to! This measure is a *last resort*.

But in practice, few interviewers will risk antagonizing future employees by such pressure tactics. In almost every case where this happens, it turns out that the interviewee has not established his or her credentials properly, and the interviewer has made no mental commitment to the person being considered.

All of the foregoing falls apart when you are negotiating a salary with the employer's *agent*, whether it is a recruiter, a personnel department employee, or another type of middleman. You can be successful *only* when you are negotiating with the person for whom you will be directly working, or who has ultimate decision-making power with regard to hiring you. If you are talking with anyone else, you should politely decline to answer any salary questions and, instead, demonstrate a genuine interest to find out more about the job and to meet the person to whom you would be reporting on the job.

If you find that the best salary offer you can negotiate is not entirely satisfactory, but you still would like to accept the job offer, you should communicate your reservations with regard to salary while showing your interest in the job, and then ask for a commitment to review your salary in six months *based on your demonstrated value.* In Chapter 13, "The Internal Campaign," you will learn how to demonstrate value in a job.

Avoid discussion of fringe benefits until you have received and negotiated a firm salary offer. Fringe benefits tend to be standard throughout an organization. Everyone gets them and, except for a few things like stock options, etc., they tend not to be negotiable.

Compensation other than salary does not apply to every job offer, but should be considered in most cases. You should know and understand the organization's fringe benefit package. Frequently, in positions where travel is required, a car will be supplied by the company. In senior positions, stock options are sometimes available. If neither of these is offered, they can frequently be negotiated as special incentives. Ask for anything that would enable you to do a better job. Make sure, as stated above, that you are *not* given benefits *instead of salary;* only after you have negotiated the highest salary offer possible should you discuss other benefits.

In the case of a commission-compensated job, you can frequently ask for special incentive bonus arrangements. Such requests show your high productivity expectation and will be music to your future employer's ear.

Remember, it is difficult to negotiate anything once you have accepted the offer. Make sure you have considered and negotiated all possible factors of employment *before* saying yes.

You will have your own order of priorities, but here are some considerations that people often miss in the rush to accept (or to reject) a job offer:

- Is the job description clear? (duties, responsibilities, authority)
- What are the opportunities for advancement? What is your employer's attitude toward advancement?
- How long has the position been in existence? Or open?
- What happened to your predecessors, if any, in the position ?
- Who are the people with whom you will be working? Have you met them?
- What is the organization's history?
- What are the organization's short- and long-range plans for growth?
- What is the reporting structure of the organization? Is it clear?

Make sure that you ask these questions, but ask them in the spirit of positive interest, and for the purpose of being able to cooperate better by understanding the function as well as the goals of the organization.

Before you make your final evaluation, *always* ask for a commitment by your future employer to review your salary within six months, based on your contributions. Even if it is the organization's policy to give only annual reviews, you can almost always get such a commitment. The request itself implies your intention to contribute.

After you have negotiated the highest possible salary offer, have understood the fringe benefits and all other relevant considerations, then always ask for at least twenty-four hours to make a decision. It is, and looks, unprofessional, to make a decision of such importance on the spot. And most people find that they have forgotten to ask some questions or to negotiate some part of the offer.

Every good offer is durable. Any offer that is withdrawn within twenty-four hours is not worth having.

You may have been made, or expect to be made, an offer by another organization. You can, at this point, use one offer to help you negotiate another. But this must be done with sincerity and tact. Bluffing or blackmailing techniques can leave you sitting between two chairs.

However, if you have another offer, you can say to your interviewer (before you accept his offer): "I'd like to ask your advice. I have been made another offer, and I have to make a decision." Be sure to follow up with a statement about your enthusiasm for his organization and the job he offered you. In many cases, the interviewer will provide a further incentive to make it possible for you to make a decision in his favor.

If, however, you prefer the other offer to the present one, you can ask for certain specific things that would make this one more acceptable to you.

It is customary in any organization to put an offer in writing. It is good to ask for such a written offer, because it avoids later misunderstandings.

Employment contracts are now relatively rare except in certain professions. Their advantage is more to the employer than to you. Whenever you are asked to sign a document prior to employment, such as an employment contract or a noncompetitive agreement, make sure your attorney reviews it before you sign it.

When you have made a decision to accept an offer, let your future employer know about it as soon as possible, preferably by telephone. Once you have given every aspect of an offer careful consideration, there is no reason to delay, and you will once again demonstrate your positive attitude by telephoning your employer.

It has always been a mystery to me that even people who have developed a habit of writing thank-you letters fail to write one to the person who has helped them the most by offering them a job.

So—once again—write a thank-you letter.

Let's conclude this chapter with a classic example of salary negotiations:

Undershaft: But Mr. Cusins, this is a serious matter. You are not bringing any capital into the concern.

Cusins: What! No capital! Is my mastery of Greek no capital! Is my access to subtlest thought, the loftiest poetry yet attained by humanity, no capital? My character! My intellect! My life! My career! What Barbara calls my soul! Are these no capital? Say another word and I double my salary.

Undershaft: Be reasonable—

Cusins: Mr. Undershaft, you have my terms. Take them or leave them.

Undershaft (recovering himself): Very well, I note your terms, and I offer half.

Cusins: Half!

Undershaft: Half.

Cusins: You call yourself a gentleman; and you offer me half!

Undershaft: I do not call myself a gentleman; but I offer you half.

—GEORGE BERNARD SHAW (*Major Barbara*)

This example illustrates a number of points: On the plus side, Professor Cusins was aware of his value and communicated it well. He also negotiated with an owner of the firm who had considerable flexibility and control and was not bound by corporate policy. On the minus side, Cusins gave away a figure, which was used as a starting point for a lower offer.

In the end, as you probably know, he continued and concluded his salary negotiations successfully, because his employment under favorable conditions served a mutual interest.

11
The
Long-Distance
Campaign

Your job and career choice may include relocation to other parts of the country or even to other parts of the world. This chapter describes a simple but effective system for relocating to another geographic area without losing income, without accepting a job outside of your career field, and without the uncertainty usually associated with such a move.

But note the following: This method is simple and effective only if followed *in every detail*. Shortcuts at any stage of the process will make the system useless. The long-distance campaign has been described by hundreds of our clients as often being easier and quicker than the local market campaign provided the rules are followed exactly.

For the purposes of this chapter, we will assume that you do not have unlimited financial resources, which would allow you to relocate with the aim of starting a market campaign once you have completed the move. As will become clear later, such a move may not be in your best interests, even if you could afford it.

Here is a step-by-step description of the long-distance campaign procedure:

First, decide where you want to live and work. If your geographic area of preference is a large one, such as the West

168

Coast or New England, divide it up into several industrial population centers. Then rank them in your order of preference. Conduct only *one* long-distance campaign at a time. One of your strengths during your long-distance interviews is your conscious choice of, and commitment to, a place where you want to live and work, as opposed to a more or less accidental condition of residence. If your preference is for a large area of the country, and your actual choice of a city or town has yet to be made, your commitment is hard to prove and your energy will be scattered and diluted. So target your efforts precisely. You can always plan and carry out a second long-distance campaign to another area based on the information you gathered on your first one.

The second step of your long-distance campaign is, paradoxically, a limited Referral campaign where you now live. The purpose of this is twofold.

One, you must be absolutely certain that you are familiar with the techniques of the Referral interview and can achieve its purposes. The relatively short time available for a long-distance campaign will not allow you to get on-the-job training for your interview technique. Make sure you know how to establish rapport with interviewers, get the kind of advice and information you need, ask for and receive referrals, and leave interviewers with a favorable impression of you. A minimum of six interviews is required for this interview training, using the methods described in Chapter 6.

Two, obtain information on your chosen target area. Because your stated purpose is to relocate, this will be the information you will be seeking. You will be amazed, as all our clients are, at the amount of dormant information people have about your chosen part of the country.

One of the aims of your local campaign will be to identify, and be referred to, people whose organizations have branches in your target area or who do business with similar organizations there. The majority of our clients have received a number of personal referrals to their relocation areas.

While you are conducting your limited local campaign, you will be conducting a research program, designed to identify people and organizations that play a key role in the community in which you plan to live.

The following is an outline of your research program:

Subscribe to the major newspaper in the area, as well as any local trade, civic, or other publications.

Write to the executive director of the chamber of commerce, asking for printed information about your target area. You can find out the director's name from your local chamber of commerce or by calling long distance. Remember, always deal with people, not with organizations. In your letter, give the reasons for your decision to move to the area and to live and work there. Enclose your resume for informational purposes. The response to such requests has varied over the years, but in most cases, the information supplied by chambers of commerce has proven to be a gold mine. Most of the printed materials are free of charge. A number of industrial directories are also frequently available at low cost.

Some of your information will, of course, come from your local Referral contacts. Some of it may come from people you already know or know of who live in the area of your choice. Having some contacts in your target area is not a requirement, although sometimes it is a bonus.

The purpose of this research is, again, twofold: First, it forms the basis for your first approach to specifically identified individuals when you are ready to start your long-distance campaign. Second, it demonstrates your commitment to the area of the country in which your interviewer lives. It is the basis for much of the rapport you will establish during your interview.

The Next Step is to schedule a trip to your target area. Give yourself about two months lead time to complete your correspondence with potential interviewers. If you are working, your vacation is an ideal time to plan such a trip. We have found that people who consider their vacation time too valuable to use for this purpose should carefully review their commitment to making a move at all!

Your carefully planned trip should last at least two weeks. Two and a half or three weeks is even better. In some cases, your correspondence will generate an invitation to make the trip at the expense of a potential employer, but it is safer to assume that you will be paying your own expenses. Second trips to the same area, if necessary, are frequently financed by prospective employers.

You are now ready to send out your first round of letters. Send these letters to key people in business and the community in your target area, such as:

- Presidents or senior executives of major companies, including, but not limited to, those in your career field.
- Civic leaders and directors of professional organizations, such as Rotary clubs, YMCAs and YWCAs, business and professional men's and women's clubs.
- Religious leaders, even if you're not affiliated with a church or synagogue.
- Educators, presidents of universities or other educational institutions or systems.
- Government leaders at the local, state, and federal levels, including members of Congress.
- People you know or have been referred to.

Write a minimum of twenty-four letters. If you don't know of that many people, continue your local interview and research activities until you do.

This long-distance letter is the only instance of a letter asking the recipient to take follow-through initiative. It should contain the following:

You (and your spouse) have decided to relocate to. . . .

In order to decide on timing and to make specific plans, you need information only a person in the recipient's position can give.

You don't expect the recipient of this letter to know of specific opportunities, but you would like information about the business climate, job market trends, and the community as a place to live and work.

You are aware that the recipient is a busy person and you would appreciate a reply, however brief, to your questions. This will help you make important decisions with regard to your move and enable you to plan a visit to his or her city.

Enclose a resume as a matter of courtesy and information.

It is assumed that at this point you do not know most or all of the people to whom you will send such letters.

Experience shows that the majority of the recipients reply to such a letter. It is a reasonable and courteous request for information, and it acknowledges that the other person is in a position to know this information. Some of the responses may take a while to arrive. This is the reason for allowing two months for this process to be completed.

Once you have received responses to better than half of the letters you send out, you will be ready to start mailing your second round of letters. They should go to all those people who have responded to your first letter, *regardless* of the nature of the response. Most of your respondents will agree that their city is a good one to live and work in. Some will describe possible difficulties in locating the right job, which can be taken as a sign of sincere concern. If those people didn't care about you and your plans, they would not have responded at all.

These second letters should follow the format of the Referral letter outlined in the chapter titled "Building Communications":

- Thank the addressee for his or her response to your letter.
- Reaffirm your commitment to both your career objective and your decision to move to his or her area.
- Give the dates of your planned visit.
- Write that, on your arrival, you will telephone to set up an appointment with him or her.
- Again, state that you don't expect him or her to know of a specific opportunity.
- Enclose another copy of your resume; don't assume that the recipient has your resume still on his desk.

There is a world of difference between a decision to *consider* a move and the decision to *make* a move. No one will commit time and resources to helping you until they are sure you have made a decision. This isn't to say that you cannot change your decision, if the information you receive makes it advisable to do so. But there has to be a commitment on your part, and it has to be stated in no uncertain terms.

The Next Step is the trip to your target area. Prepare to spend the entire time on a concentrated market campaign. Resist the temptation to indulge in side trips, sightseeing, or other vacation activities. You will need to be at the top of your form, mentally and physically. Get lots of sleep, eat well, take extra time to review your accomplishments and assets, and prepare for your interviews. You can leave the writing of thank-you letters until you return home, if necessary.

As soon as you arrive and have checked into your hotel or

other lodging, start telephoning all the people to whom you wrote. Have a calendar handy in which to schedule your appointments.

Expect to schedule three appointments each day, no more, no less, including Saturdays, and even Sundays, if possible. The first appointment should always be first thing in the morning, the second right after lunch. In some cases, make luncheon appointments, if that is convenient. Lunch or dinner interviews can be very productive, if they are not drowned in alcohol. Note that the person issuing the invitation is expected to pay for the meal! The third interview should be scheduled from mid to late afternoon or early evening.

Three interviews a day is all you can handle and still be in good form. Less is a waste of your valuable time.

Follow the interview procedure outlined in Chapter 6, with one exception: It is permissible to skip the letter of approach to persons to whom you are being referred. You may set up the interview by telephone, or even ask the person who referred you to set it up for you, if you have excellent rapport with him or her. Most people will make an extra effort to be helpful in response to your demonstrated extra effort to travel to their city.

Leave at least two full days open at the end of your trip to follow up referrals you are given. In fact, you may find yourself receiving so many referrals that you have to make a choice between following them up or seeing people with whom you have previously scheduled interviews. Everything else being equal, personal referrals are usually more valuable, especially if they are in your career field. It is perfectly all right to cancel a previously set appointment, provided you telephone the person you expected to see and explain that your schedule is heavier than anticipated. Thank the person for making the time available and say that you would like to meet him or her in the future. Then, reiterate this in a thank-you letter. He or she will understand.

If you have followed the above outline, you should receive a show of interest from several organizations. This does not necessarily have to be in the form of firm job offers. It is normal either to be invited back for a second interview at the company's expense or to receive a job offer in the mail or by telephone.

You may, however, get involved in serious negotiations, at least to the point of discussing relocation expenses. This is not as sensitive an issue as it may seem. Most large organizations have provisions for relocation expenses and don't consider them to be a major factor in hiring decisions. Smaller organizations may suggest a compromise and limit their expense compensation. This then becomes just one of the items to be negotiated. The timing and method for such negotiations are described in Chapter 10.

In some cases, it may be advantageous for you to offer to pay relocation expenses in return for a higher salary offer, even if this means you will have to take out a loan. Remember, the salary increment is paid every year, relocation expenses are paid only once.

More about travel expenses: Who pays and when?

Normally, the person who initiates the meeting is expected to pay the expenses. If you receive an invitation for an interview, the organization with which you are interviewing will pay the expenses, unless otherwise stated. Sometimes you are invited to come in "when you are in the area." This means the organization does not expect to pay any expenses.

If you request a meeting, and the organization simply responds to your request, they are under no obligation to pay your expenses and frequently won't. However, it is easy to eliminate any mystery by asking, "Will you pay my travel expenses?" Or you can make it stronger by saying, "I assume you will pay my travel expenses." In any case, clarification in advance will eliminate unpleasant surprises.

To summarize this chapter, I will quote from a letter sent to us by a woman who had completed a long-distance campaign, relocating from Washington, D.C., to Chicago:

> I hope I can offer some insight into the methods, techniques, resources, and problems, etc., which I used or encountered in my long-distance campaign, and more important, why I was successful. I have spent a great deal of time thinking about this and examining all aspects of my market campaign. I will try to highlight those elements which we worked on together to make the whole process work.
>
> Motivation, determination, and hard work are what makes a job campaign a success, whether it is local or long-distance. But in some respects, I think the long-distance campaign is easier. First of all, you must concentrate your efforts into a given span of time: No room for goofing off. You must be UP, mentally, and completely prepared because you are investing time and money into your effort (unless you are lucky enough to get someone else to pay for your trip). Also, it is *all* you are doing for a set number of days. On a local campaign, you can be more casual and more often than not, I would assume you are interspersing the Referral interviews with other activities. On a long-distance campaign, the Referral interviews are *all* you are thinking about.
>
> You should leave no stone unturned in seeking Referral interviews. People whom you have forgotten years ago will remember you and want to help. I found a great willingness on the part of Referrals to help, once I mentioned how much I loved Chicago. It confirmed their own happiness about living here.
>
> Preparation for the Referral interviews is an essential component. You must be prepared for each interview. If you are not, you are wasting a valuable contact and wasting your time as

well. People do want to help and they are even more inclined if they feel you are serious about yourself and your goals.

Don't get discouraged. Even an interview that bombs can produce a positive action. And thank-you notes do count and can make the difference. I know one of mine turned a mediocre interview into a solid lead.

Also, there must be a willingness to do the work. More important, you must be honest with yourself when you are doing the work—no cutting corners. Each work task is part of the whole puzzle, and when it all comes together, that is when the long-distance campaign program works for you.

Now that I have gone through this, is a long-distance campaign so different from a local one? Probably not.

Remember: A person's commitment to a job is an important factor in hiring decisions, because it reduces the employer's risk. People who relocate are often viewed favorably, because they demonstrate their commitment by making a financial and emotional investment in the area to which they move.

12
Your New Job: Career Follow-Through

Now that you are in your new job, the exciting task of career building begins. Your new job is an opportunity! Nothing more and nothing less. It all depends on you: What you do on the first day, the first week, and the first month decides whether the job is a temporary assignment or a solid part of your career.

Earlier I have said that business is people. This fact takes on extra significance at this point. The relationship you establish with your associates and superiors during the first days of your new job will decide your future in the job.

Understanding a few principles governing all relationships between people is all you need to know to get started right. In this chapter I will discuss those human relations principles and show you how to apply them.

Two of the major factors in human relations are emotions and communications. An understanding of these two factors and how they interact is essential to the establishment of positive interpersonal relationships. Because the role feelings play is crucial to all forms of human interaction, I will deal with feelings first.

There is no such thing as complete objectivity, just as there is no such thing as an action or reaction completely governed by feelings.

178

All human thought and action are colored by feelings, positive or negative. In fact, feelings can never be neutral. A positive feeling can put steam behind an idea. It can supply the power necessary to put the idea into practice. For example, a career objective is an idea. To the extent that you have positive emotions involved in that idea, you will be successful, sometimes against considerable odds.

To the extent that a rational concept is affected by feelings, its validity is diminished. For instance, time and size are rational concepts which feelings make into mincemeat. An event invested with negative feelings appears to take much more time than an accurate measurement reveals. When someone is late for a meeting with you, your feeling may tell you you've been waiting for an hour, while your watch may show that you have waited only ten minutes. Conversely, a pleasant event is over much too soon.

Feelings are responsible for fueling both short-term and long-term trends in human relationships. The concept of positive and negative emotional trends, as well as other human relations covered in this chapter, were developed by Eli Djeddah, noted educator and author.

All your actions and words affect others around you. To the degree that others' perceptions of what you do or say are colored by their feelings, their responses are also colored by these same feelings, positive or negative. This response does not necessarily depend on whether the original action or statement had any emotional content.

For instance, if I offer a promotion to an employee, I may have made a rational decision (keeping in mind that there is no such thing; I should say, a *relatively* rational decision). The employee communicates that pleasure by his actions and words. This in turn produces feelings of pleasure in me, not the least of which is validation of, and reward for, my original action.

I now have a positive relationship with this employee. Some

of the possible benefits from this relationship are increased effort by the employee in my behalf and motivation on my part to further acknowledge and reward the employee. This is a positive trend that can continue unless something blocks it. It is important to see that the positive trend was produced by initiatives on both our parts. The employee earned the promotion, and I decided to give it. If either one, or both of us, had failed to take these initiatives, a negative trend might have been started. If either the employee had failed to do a good job or I had failed to acknowledge it, negative feelings would have been generated and responded to. Eventually this might have led to a breakdown of communications, dismissal, or the employee's decision to leave the firm.

Starting a positive trend requires action, while inaction can produce a negative trend. Remember, feelings can't be neutral. The only people about whom we don't have positive *or* negative feelings are people we don't care about one way or the other.

How can you learn to recognize and control emotional reactions?

Become increasingly aware to what extent an action or statement is rational, and to what extent it is emotional. You then can learn to adjust your responses accordingly.

For instance, as counselors we frequently deal with clients who have just been fired. Very likely a client in this situation is heavily affected by strong negative emotions. It would be useless to respond only to the part of the situation that can be dealt with on the rational level and give the client a set of rational instructions. We must also be aware of the client's emotional state and respond to it. If we don't do that, we are of no more value to the client than a piece of cardboard full of printed instructions.

Remember that your own attitudes and responses to others are colored by your emotions. They are affected by the entire spectrum of feelings from admiration, liking, and respect, to boredom, resentment, blame, and sometimes hostility.

Learn to recognize these feelings and channel them. Whenever a negative emotion or an increasingly negative trend threatens your relationship with another person at work, *take the initiative in building a positive trend.* Your feelings cannot help you in this. You have to call on your reason to decide where and how to start this positive trend.

The following is an example of a negative trend:

I'm your boss. I forget to say good morning to you one day. You react negatively and retaliate by not speaking to me for the rest of the day. I retaliate by not giving you a deserved raise. You stop working hard and come in late every day. I fire you. By this time, no one even remembers how the trend started.

Now an example for a similar positive trend:

I go out of my way to praise your work. You work even harder. I give you an extra raise. You look for every way to aid me in my work and become an exemplary employee. I give you a promotion. It's as simple as that!

You can learn to control positive or negative trends, including trends resulting from quick, largely emotional reactions to an event or statement. Usually, the longer the reaction is delayed, the greater the chance of making a balanced response. A good response is one that either avoids the danger of starting a negative trend or builds a positive one.

An understanding of emotions is extremely valuable in the area of prejudice. Whenever you prejudge a person or a situation, you do so partly on the rational and partly on the emotional level. On the *rational* level, there is a tendency to extrapolate from the information you have to the information you don't have—making an educated guess. On the emotional level, you may fill a need or follow a pattern of your own.

A good example is a client, Norman T., who came to us

after his research firm had failed. It had been his practice to employ only people with advanced degrees. In analyzing this policy, he came to the following conclusions: On the rational level, he was convinced that people with academic certification were more likely to be intelligent, more disciplined, and more capable than people without it. To him this was only common sense. On the emotional level, Norman felt that his own investment in academic training and certification would be diminished if he hired anyone who had not made the same investment.

Norman's prejudice (which he finally recognized) has led him to disqualify many potential employees with important business experience and ultimately led to the downfall of the company.

Once you understand the nature of prejudice, you are in a position to analyze your thoughts and feelings and channel them into constructive action.

Responding to a negative emotional statement or action with another negative emotional statement or action is natural, easy, and entirely destructive.

To do this at work will start or reinforce a negative trend and will seriously damage your work environment. The satisfaction it generates is short-term at best, whereas the negative trend will keep building until your relationship with the other person is severed completely, or one of you takes the initiative to build a positive trend.

Don't fight fire with fire; fight fire with water. The only way to stop a negative emotional trend is to replace it with a positive one. However, building a positive trend is difficult. It must be learned and practiced often.

If you accept that the world of work is a world of people, you must communicate with people in order to do your work. All activities that are part of your work become meaningful only when you interact with people, and you cannot interact unless you communicate.

A person who has a good reason to hear what you say will always listen. When you communicate information that is to the listener's benefit (from his or her point of view), you will always be heard. If the information you give will diminish the listener, either it will not be heard at all, or it will cause a negative reaction.

Sometimes a statement diminishes and benefits the listener at the same time. This can happen when an ultimatum is given. For example, a valuable employee comes to me and says: "You are not paying me enough, and if you don't give me a raise, I'll quit." I now stand accused of unfairness, but I also find that it may be to my benefit to meet the demand and approve the raise. The employee is taking a gamble and, for all practical purposes, has lost control of the situation. Even if I give in to solve the short-range problem, I will take steps to avoid being placed in a similar situation in the future. The employee may have initiated a negative trend, which may escalate and eventually end in disaster for the employee. Experience and statistics show that this is what usually happens.

Experience also shows that when you establish a positive emotional climate, you open many channels of communication. What is a positive emotional climate? It is a climate that is beneficial to the person with whom you wish to communicate. If you want to establish positive communications, first listen to the other person in order to find his or her wavelength.

For example, communications problems usually arise when someone lodges a complaint. Normally, a complaint phrased in negative terms tends to accuse and diminish the recipient. (An emotional complaint can, of course, bring relief to the complainer's feelings; but it will rarely produce long-range change for the better in the situation that brought about the complaint in the first place.) The recipient of the complaint will have the following emotional reaction: "If you are on my side, I'll listen; if you are against me, I won't listen."

This points the way to lodging a successful complaint: You must form an alliance with the other person in order to find a solution. If you don't, you will be seen as a nuisance and either ignored or received with hostility.

Your ability to establish communications with your fellow human beings is closely related to your attitude toward them.

A client once called me and said that his boss had not spoken to him for three consecutive days. He asked if that meant his boss had taken a sudden dislike to him and perhaps intended to fire him. Our client was well on his way toward retaliation and was even considering handing in his resignation to head off being fired. Among other things, this illustrates the inability of the emotions to perceive shades of gray. To this client, in his emotional state, it was all or nothing! It turned out that the boss had a personal problem that had nothing to do with our client's work but which prevented the boss from communicating in a normal way.

Finally, give some thought to nonverbal communications. The effect of a friendly attitude is often far more powerful than words. Because of the black and white nature of our emotions, the absence of a friendly attitude can have devastating consequences.

Once you understand the importance of positive and negative trends in communications, you can start applying the following twelve rules for moving ahead in your job. Our clients have learned and applied these rules successfully for many years.

One—START EACH DAY'S WORK WITH A SMILE. MAINTAIN
GOOD PHYSICAL HEALTH, AN ATTRACTIVE
APPEARANCE, AND A POSITIVE ATTITUDE.

Starting each day (including Mondays) with a smile sounds like an easy thing to do. It is! Try it for a week. The return on your investment will be considerable. Maintaining good health, insofar as you have control over your health, is one of the ingredients of being considered a successful and dynamic person. The fact that you have a large measure of control over your state of health is increasingly recognized by the medical profession, and preventive medicine and health maintenance are now accepted concepts. An attractive appearance is within everyone's means.

Maintaining a positive attitude, especially in the face of a variety of problems, is not always easy. Sometimes it requires effort. To the extent that you make a habit of maintaining an increasingly positive attitude toward the people you work with, you will be in control of your work environment. Progress in this area pays large dividends, even in small increments.

Two—TAKE THE INITIATIVE IN TREATING OTHERS AS YOU WOULD LIKE TO BE TREATED.

This rule is well known to everyone, at least in theory. Applying it is another matter. The operative part of this rule is: Take the initiative. Most people only react to their treatment by others, which means turning control over to the person who takes the initiative. Make sure you are the one who sets the tone of your relationships with others.

Three—KNOW YOUR ORGANIZATION'S GOALS AND PURPOSES SO YOU CAN ALIGN YOUR EFFORTS WITH THOSE OF YOUR EMPLOYER.

Your work will be rewarded only insofar as it contributes to your employer's goals. Hard work in itself is no virtue. In fact, it may demonstrate your inefficiency. Make sure your goals in your work are in line with those of your employer.

How do you know? Ask him! This information will be freely given and your desire to be informed will be seen as a plus. If it is impossible for you to share your employer's purposes with enthusiasm, you are in the wrong job or even in the wrong career.

Four—STUDY THE SUCCESSFUL PEOPLE IN YOUR
ORGANIZATION. SEEK THEIR ADVICE.

It will take you very little time in a new job to find out who is considered able and successful in your company. Associate with these people. Ignore the disgruntled employees who gather like sediment at the bottom of every organization. These people are in the wrong job, and they don't have the courage to do something about it. Once you have become a vital part of the organization, you may even be able to help some of those people by sharing with them the principles of sound career planning.

Five—TAKE TIME TO CONSIDER PROBLEMS BEFORE TAKING
ACTION. AVOID INSTANT EMOTIONAL REACTIONS.

At the emotional or feeling level, no one is mature. It is our ability to think and reason that gives us maturity. Instant reactions are, therefore, almost always immature. If they are negative, they can do a lot of damage. In a second's time, you may unwittingly lay the groundwork for a long-term negative trend in your relationship with another person.

This is not to say that you should leave problems unresolved. But it does mean that you should make sure you have given yourself enough time to consider the nature of the response, so you can stay in control of the situation. *There is always time.*

Six—NEVER PRESENT A PROBLEM WITHOUT SUGGESTING A
CONSTRUCTIVE SOLUTION.

It may appear practical to unload problems on the person who is paid to solve them or who is most suited to deal with them. But from a human relations point of view, it is considered a negative action. If the problem is presented in the nature of a complaint, it actually serves to diminish the recipient, as described earlier.

By suggesting a solution, even if it isn't the best possible one, you have demonstrated your willingness to take part of the responsibility. In the case of a complaint, you have taken the sting of blame out of it. Complaining and blaming are purely emotional actions and will almost always generate negative emotional reactions.

Seven—COMMUNICATE YOUR CONTRIBUTIONS AND
ACCOMPLISHMENTS TO YOUR EMPLOYER.
RECOGNIZE THE CONTRIBUTIONS OF OTHERS.

Your employer has a job of his own. Recognizing and acknowledging your personal contributions is only a small part of this job. This isn't a personal slight, although at the emotional level it is often perceived as such, because the feelings do not recognize shades of gray. Far from being demeaning, communicating your contributions to your superior is a way to help him do his job better.

When you have people under you, it is often necessary to encourage them to report their contributions to you periodically. This generates several benefits: You will be perceived as a fair employer. Your subordinates will sharpen their awareness of what is, and what is not, a genuine contribution and will thereby become more effective in their work. And morale as well as productivity will increase.

If there is no system for this in the organization in which you work, make a positive impact by initiating a regular progress reporting system. No matter what your position in the organization, your initiative in reporting your progress will be welcomed and rewarded, provided it is compatible with your job description.

Our client, Barbara D., had recently accepted a position as

art director in a publishing company. During her first weeks on the job, she found out that the salaries of the art department were reviewed once a year and the requests for increases submitted to management were automatically cut in half. We helped Barbara formulate a plan for bringing about a change.

In talking with the executive responsible for salary decisions, she learned that he had only a vague idea about what the art department did. Barbara asked each of the people in her department to submit a brief, written summary of the contributions he or she had made during the year since the last salary review. She then compiled a progress report, giving one or two major contributions for each employee. When she submitted this report together with a request for salary increases, the increases were approved without cuts. This represented a change in an unwritten company policy of eighty-five years' standing. It was brought about by the constructive initiative of one person.

Eight—ESTABLISH A REPUTATION FOR DOING YOUR
ASSIGNMENTS WELL AND ON TIME.

If you have a reputation for reliability, you will be given more chances for advancement, assuming you observe rule number seven and communicate the results of your work to your superior. Such a reputation has to be built step by step. The cumulative effect can be powerful.

Nine—WHEN YOU ARE IN CONTROL OF YOUR JOB, ADD
NEW RESPONSIBILITY WITH YOUR SUPERIOR'S
AGREEMENT.

You are responsible for advancement in your job and career. The evidence for this is overwhelming, yet most people abdicate this responsibility completely. It is either fate, luck, or the boss who is held responsible.

Advancement is a matter of building on a solid foundation. The fact that you have been in the job for a certain length of time is not a good reason for expecting advancement.

Make sure you are in control of your job and have produced solid results. Then ask to be given additional responsibilities which are within your power to carry out and are in line with your employer's purposes. If you make a convincing case for taking on extra duties, you will have no problem getting your employer's agreement. After you have carried out the new responsibilities for a period of time, you can use this as a basis for a salary increase and other recognition.

Ten—PLAN THE NEXT STEP IN YOUR JOB AND CAREER. NEVER BE WITHOUT ACHIEVABLE GOALS.

Planning your Next Step is a means of setting a goal for your current assignment. If you know what the requirements are, in terms of knowledge and experience for your Next Step, you can use your time and energy efficiently in your current job to gain that knowledge and experience. Again, you will be successful only if you benefit your employer and yourself alike. One *or* the other is of no value.

Eleven—CONTINUE YOUR FORMAL OR INFORMAL EDUCATION; NEVER STOP LEARNING AND GROWING.

A job rarely provides all the opportunites for personal and professional growth automatically. On the other hand, formal academic education does not always automatically increase your abilities and opportunities for professional growth.

Use your career objectives as the main point of reference in planning your continuing education. Your Success Factors are a sure guide to this.

One of the greatest misuses of time and energy is the notion that one should educate oneself in an area of weakness or disinclination to somehow raise the average level of ability. This is patent nonsense. The same time and energy spent on further education and growth in an area in which you have a basic strength, inclination, and enthusiasm will produce ten times more growth!

If I like numbers and mathematics and I have enjoyed bookkeeping jobs, then experience and education probably will help me to build a successful career as an accountant, perhaps leading to a business of my own or a corporation controllership. If I detest numbers and adding a column of figures is a traumatic experience for me, I will never even become competitive in applying for an assistant bookkeeper's job, no matter how many accounting courses I take.

Twelve—CONTINUE BUILDING AND COMMUNICATING WITH YOUR CONTACT NETWORK.

Periodically write to the people you have met during your market campaign. Keep them informed about your progress, and share information with them. If you read an article about an important event in your field, clip it or make a copy and send it to those members of your contact network with whom you have a common interest.

You have worked hard to build this network; it is relatively simple to keep it alive. You will need people throughout your career. Make sure you have access to them at any time by staying in touch. In addition, make sure you become aware of everyone who has made a major contribution in your field or who holds a key position. Develop the habit of screening all information that comes to you through print and broadcast media, as well as word of mouth, for the names of people you can add to your contact network.

These twelve rules are the result of a Success Factor Analysis performed on thousands of successful Haldane clients. Successful people practice these rules daily. An easy way to join this exclusive club is to write these rules on a piece of paper and carry them with you until you have made them a daily habit.

How do you use all the above information to get started in your new job? The following is a step-by-step guide.

Use your first week to set up communications with the people with whom you will be working. Start on your very first day in the job. Many months and perhaps years of working relationships may depend on how well you do this.

There is a tendency in each of us to prove ourselves during the first days on a job, to justify our employer's decision to hire us, to fulfill his expectations.

Resist the temptation to be the new broom that sweeps clean. Remember that every person in the organization has been on the job longer than you have. They know more about the company than you do. By discounting this prior knowledge, regardless of whether it is fact or feeling, you diminish others and may well plant the seed for a long-term negative emotional climate. Conversely, if you acknowledge a person's seniority by enlisting his or her help in getting started in your job and getting to know the organization, you will ensure a positive trend and lay the groundwork for a constructive relationship. You will have opened a channel of communications.

You will not be expected to produce tangible results in most jobs during the first weeks or months. This is an ideal time for establishing open relationships with the key people in your organization.

It is also a good time to meet all the people at every level of the organization who have a bearing on your job and your career advancement. Take the initiative to see them and to gain an understanding of their purposes and goals. Offer your commitment to contribute to the achievement of their goals. You may never have such an opportunity again. This kind of initiative is always welcome in a new employee.

After you have been in the job for about a week, start making an organizational diagram. Some larger organizations publish such diagrams, but it is to your advantage to assemble one for yourself. It will help you to become aware of the structure of the organization in which you are working. Published organizational totem poles are usually not a clear reflection of the true lines of authority. The research you do to construct such a diagram will give you an in-depth understanding of how your organization functions. It will be valuable material for planning your career advancement when the time comes.

In addition to such a diagram, make a list of key people in the organization, insofar as you have contact with them. Write a brief description of each of these people and keep adding to them as you get to know them better. Write down anything you think is important to know about them, including their name, title, job description (as you see it), length of time with the organization, personality characteristics, as well as likes and dislikes. This description helps you to understand the organizational environment as well as the people environment in which you work, which are key prerequisites for being in tune with the organization and advancing within it.

Before the end of the first month, start a log of your contributions. A diary-type book allowing daily or weekly entries is ideal for this purpose. Write down, in telegram style, everything that could remotely be called an achievement or a contribution, large or small. When the time is right, this record will become the basis for a presentation to your superiors, asking for an increase in salary or a promotion. In fact, every kind of on-the-job career advancement must be based on achievement, in order to be successful. But no one will remember all of your achievements, not even you.

Example: A client of ours joined a very conservative insurance firm as an administrative assistant. She negotiated a commitment for a six-month review of her salary. After three months she reviewed her achievement log. Due to a flu epidemic, she had done not only her own job, but the work of a number of other people as well. She felt that the original six-month period should be reduced. Accordingly, she wrote a letter to her boss listing several dozen contributions. The boss had gained an overall impression that she was always available when needed, but had been too busy himself to acknowledge it in any tangible way. When he had read her letter, he called her into his office and said, "I had no idea you did all these things!" He promoted her to a full administrator's position and gave her an increase in salary retroactive to her starting date.

In Chapter 13 you will learn exactly how to go about making such a presentation and the timing involved in getting the desired results.

It is assumed that you have a fair understanding of what is expected of you in the performance of your duties, but job descriptions are rarely accurate and change periodically. Your own personality will influence how your job is being done. After the first few months, your job description may in fact have changed considerably without your being aware of it. This is why you must review your job description with your superior after no more than three months in the job.

So after three months, write down a description of your job, and ask your boss to do the same. You will be amazed how much the two job descriptions differ. This is normal. It also underlines the necessity for reviewing job descriptions and expectations periodically. This divergence of job expectations is the major reason that salary increases and promotions fail to materialize. All of our clients are engaged on a continuous program of communicating with their superiors about the nature and structure of their jobs.

13
The Internal Campaign

Now that you have been in your job long enough to become familiar with it, what is your Next Step? If you have't received the recognition, the advancement, the income you feel you have earned, what is your Next Step? If you've outgrown your job, what's your Next Step? Even if you don't like your job anymore, there are Next Steps other than looking elsewhere for a new job.

The best opportunities may be with your present employer. The position you now hold gives you a strategic vantage point for career advancement, and you should not be reluctant to make the most of it.

There are three job improvement advantages you have in your present company. First, you have access to people in the organization who can help you determine what your company needs to increase profitability. Second, by identifying needs, you can put yourself in a position to help make priority contributions to your organization. Finally, our experience has shown that organizations like to promote from within any time they believe the move will upgrade their operations or staff. Someone who knows the organization has more potential value to the firm than a new employee who must be broken in, provided the staff member knows how to demonstrate his or her value. We have also found that employers are willing to pay attractive salaries to those who can make productive contributions to the organization.

Even though this positive environment for career growth exists, most employees don't go after internal advancement in the right way. Instead they usually go by one of two routes: talking to their boss or waiting for something to happen. Both are ineffective.

Talking to your boss about recognition raises your personal problem to a supervisor who has problems of his or her own. It is likely to get lost among other issues awaiting action. Waiting for a promotion presupposes that management has both the time and the motivation to observe and reward every employee's contributions. Although this does happen occasionally, you have no control over the timing and the nature of the recognition. That is why we recommend conducting an Internal campaign.

The Internal campaign is a concept developed by Bernard Haldane Associates many years ago. Because this concept is based on sound principles of human relations, it *always* produces a positive response, provided the simple rules described below are followed.

The Internal campaign parallels an "external" job search in that it consists of setting an objective, preparing a presentation, and making contacts with those who can help you implement your objective. The Internal campaign is, however, much easier to conduct, because both the information you need and the people you will be dealing with are much more accessible to you.

Here is a step-by-step outline of an Internal campaign:

1. Conduct research.
2. Set an objective.
3. Prepare a presentation.

4. Make contact.
5. Follow through.

In order to set a realistic objective, you must have information. Be completely aware of what your organization does, what its goals are, and how it goes about reaching those goals. Some of this information is available in print, in company brochures and public relations materials. You can get most of it from people in your organization. Don't hesitate to ask for information. No one will resent your curiosity and your interest in becoming better informed about the organization in which you work, if it is motivated by positive and constructive purposes.

If you haven't already done so, draw up an organizational diagram. If a printed organizational chart is available in your organization, you might use it as a starting point. In addition to the official reporting structure, be sure to indicate the real lines of power and communications as you see them. This will allow you to take a closer look at the way your organization works and will help you avoid dead ends in your Internal campaign.

In addition, and to help you take a closer look at the people involved in making the organization function, write up brief, thumbnail descriptions of the key people in your organization, insofar as you interact with them, or expect to interact with them in the future. Remember, organizations are composed of people. In achieving anything worthwhile, you will be dealing with people, not organizations. There is no such thing as management, only people in managerial positions.

Include the following in your thumbnail descriptions: name, title, age (guess if you don't know), job description (what they are actually doing), strengths, weaknesses (as you observe them), avocations (this is usually easy to discover), and anything else that would make it easy to establish communications with the person. Try to be as objective as you can. If you find that a description of a person tends toward the negative, you may have allowed negative emotions to control your observations. Try to balance the picture by deliberately looking for positive attributes and strengths in that person.

With the help of the above information evaluate your choices and set a job objective which, though it may be ambitious, would be a genuine career advancement for you. You will later "reality-test" it, and there is always time to modify your objective. So start out with the most closely ideal job objective possible within the framework of the organization that employs you.

Your choices include promotion, a new position created for you, transfer to another department (laterally or upward), an increase in responsibility as well as authority, a new title, eliminating or delegating unwanted duties, and, of course, an increase in salary or other income and benefits.

Some of our clients have achieved multiple Internal campaign goals, such as a complete reorganization of their company, together with a new job, a new title, and increased income. For your first Internal campaign, however, I suggest starting with a more modest objective. Once you have made a habit of conducting Internal campaigns, you will be surprised how much you can accomplish.

If your objective includes a change of your job description, recheck your Success Factors (Chapter 4) to make sure they are in line with your proposed objective.

If you have a problem setting realistic objectives, or if you need more information, identify a person at a senior level in the organization, but not involved in the chain of command with regard to your position or objective, and ask for advice off the record and on a personal basis. This advice is usually given freely, because you have recognized the advice giver as having knowledge and judgment.

Preparing a presentation is an important step in the Internal campaign process. If it is omitted, failure is pretty well guaranteed! The purpose of a written presentation is to organize the facts you will be presenting for consideration and action by your superiors. It will also make it possible to bring your positive emotions in line with your objectives and prevent hostile feelings from obstructing your Internal campaign. Once you have written a positive, powerful presentation of your objective and reasons why your employer should accept it, you will be ready to implement your Internal campaign.

Your presentation should be prepared in the form of a letter or proposal. It should always be typed. The outline given below should be followed exactly, because it has been tested and retested thoroughly. It works!

PARAGRAPH 1. "Declaration of Loyalty." Because many or most letters written to superiors by employees have a negative connotation, it is essential to set a positive emotional climate by saying, in so many words, that you like the organization and the people you are working with. Your intention is to increase your contribution to the organization.

PARAGRAPH 2. In clear and concise language, state your objective. There is no point in writing a proposal in the form of a detective story, leading up to the denouement on the last page. As a courtesy, inform the reader at the outset of the reason for the letter.

PARAGRAPH 3. Support your objective by listing your accomplishments and contributions, which prove you have earned the recognition and/or are capable of carrying out the duties you are asking for. Then list the benefits your organization is likely to reap from granting your request. This is an essential factor in your presentation. If there is no benefit for the employer, you don't have a case.

The following are examples of ways to describe benefits:

- The title of Purchasing Director will enable me to deal and negotiate more effectively with vendors and suppliers.
- By combining the duties of Mrs. Miller with my own, upon her retirement, you will not only realize financial savings but will also allow me to use all my energy to benefit our company.
- By granting the recognition I ask for, you will substantially increase my motivation and my commitment to our firm. (This statement may sound self-serving, but commitment and motivation are key factors for management in considering rewards and incentives.)

If this paragraph is not powerful and convincing, you may have to go back to paragraph 2 and re-evaluate your objective.

PARAGRAPH 4. "The Human Factor." Whatever your objective is, it will affect other people in your organization. Any time your job description, responsibility level, or title is changed, this will have a bearing on other people's job descriptions. An increase in your responsibilities and authority may appear to diminish those of your superiors. It is important to consider this in preparing your presentation.

For example: If you expect to assume responsibility for some decisions that now are in your superior's area, you might point out that granting your request will allow the superior to concentrate on more important decisions. Make sure that this paragraph is realistic. There is no room for propaganda statements in your presentation.

In the case of a simple request for a salary increase, this paragraph may be omitted, though such a request has a better chance of succeeding in a big way if it is combined with an increase in responsibility.

PARAGRAPH 5. In closing, ask for an opportunity to discuss your proposal. Remember that the most efficient way to make a presentation is to make it verbally *and* in writing, not one or the other.

Give or transmit the letter to the person to whom it is addressed at a time when no instant response is possible. As you have seen, instant responses tend to be emotional, and your carefully prepared proposal deserves equally careful consideration. Many of our clients have found that Friday afternoon is a good time for presenting such a letter to a superior. If you hand the letter (in a sealed envelope) to your superior personally, you might say: "I'd like to have an opportunity to discuss this with you after you've had a chance to study it."

One firm rule in an Internal campaign is never go behind your immediate superior's back.

If your boss is the person who will make the decision, the matter is simple. If the decision is to be made by someone senior to your boss, you have a choice: You can inform your boss of your intentions and ask permission to make a presentation to the decision maker (with a copy to your boss). It can hardly be refused. If you expect your boss to be sympathetic to your cause, you can ask his advice in advance.

If, on the other hand, you expect your boss to be negative about your request, you can address your presentation to both the decision maker *and* your boss, with a copy to both simultaneously. This makes it impossible for your boss to obstruct the presentation, while you include him or her in the process.

To retain the initiative, call your superior a few days after you have transmitted your presentation and ask for a meeting to discuss it.

At such a meeting, expect a number of different reactions,

from an unconditional "yes," to a "maybe," a counterproposal, or a "no." In the case of a "maybe" or a counterproposal, you are in the negotiating position. A compromise can usually be reached. There is no need to press for a conclusion at the first meeting. Scheduling another meeting will give you time to think and to propose a compromise that will be to your advantage.

In the case of a "no," it is essential to politely but firmly ask for, and insist on, being given reasons. Your superior will usually tell you what you need to do before resubmitting a similar proposal at a later time. In a few cases, a "no" answer is an indication that you will not achieve your career advancement with your current employer and may need to look for it elsewhere. Even in these cases, the result of your Internal campaign can be positive. It gives you accurate information about your chances for career advancement. Painful as it may be, it allows you to plan your Next Step realistically.

Do not always expect results instantly. As in negotiations for a job really worth having, several meetings may be necessary to reach your goal. From your employer's point of view, timing may be an important factor in postponing a definite answer. It is essential for you to pursue the negotiation. If you allow your Internal campaign to lapse, you may convince your employer that you were not serious in the first place. This will make it much more difficult to get a response in the future.

So, an important rule of any Internal campaign is to follow it through to resolution, no matter how long it takes. This will almost guarantee success in any future Internal campaign with the same employer.

Here are a few additional ground rules for starting an Internal campaign:

Make all your communications positive. There is a natural

tendency to resent your boss because he or she has not taken more initiative in recognizing your work. Forget it! It's not an expectation justified by any known principles of human behavior. Check all of your written and verbal presentations to keep complaints and other negative emotional reactions from creeping in. However justified they may appear to you, they will create obstacles to achieving results.

Many presentations to employers start with an accusation. Such statements as "I have not received a salary increase in two years" usually elicit responses like "You haven't earned one." These useless and destructive emotional exercises are evidence of a negative trend in the making.

Once again, it is important to remember that you have to "give in order to get." A realistic objective is one that benefits *both* you and the employer, not one *or* the other only. Any Internal campaign which is not based on this principle is doomed to failure.

Another aspect of being positive is that no Internal campaign objective will succeed if it is motivated *only* by a desire to escape from a situation. A realistic objective must be a move *toward* something greater, not merely *away* from something lesser, in order to enlist the sympathy and positive response of your superiors. When you see your objective in terms of "I can't stand to work in this department—I'll go anywhere just to get away from my boss," you don't have an objective, you have a problem. When you can state it in terms of "My abilities can be used better in the X department," you are giving your employers an opportunity to benefit from your move.

The last and perhaps most important rule for starting an Internal campaign is this: Move from a position of strength! If you are behind in your work, your superior's reaction will be that you are not even able to do your present job, why would you be able to do another, or bigger one?

If you have a serious communications difficulty with your superior, you are also in a weak position to embark on a successful Internal campaign.

In both cases, make and carry out a plan to remedy the current negative situation. This means going on a personal, short-term campaign to eliminate a specific obstacle to your Internal campaign. Take the initiative to clear up any backlog in your job, and/or to communicate positively with your boss on a daily basis from four to six weeks, and then start your Internal campaign.

There are many ways to advance your career. The Internal campaign is one of the easiest and most satisfying ones available to every employed career builder.

14
Management and Leadership

The best, most ideal, and at the same time, the most realistic Internal campaign objective you can have is the one that allows you to make full use of all your strengths while minimizing the time spent on your areas of weakness and low motivation. The same is true for any career objective.

It is assumed by many that the only long-range career goal worth having is a management position. Yet, few people agree on what management is. Because the most central aspect of management is really leadership, this chapter will discuss the manager as a leader of people. Whatever the technical and administrative duties of a manager, it is skill in relating to other people at various levels that makes him or her effective.

What is leadership? Is it a skill a person is born with, or can it be learned?

If you are currently in a management position, or if you aspire to such a position as part of your career path, you will find the following definitions useful. Later in this chapter, we will give a step-by-step outline for moving into a management position.

I am using "management" in this chapter as a *job title*, i.e., a management position. "Leadership" is used as a *function*, such as leadership role, talent, skill, ability.

Leadership can be taught, given basic talent and interest.

Many people have a natural talent for it, while many others have little or none and would be desperately unhappy in a management position. Promoting even a person with leadership talent to a management position without training is very much like arranging a concert tour for an untrained person who happens to have a talent for music.

You have to learn to follow before you can lead for these reasons: The ability to follow implies an ability to listen, understand, and accept the purpose of a superior. It is no more and no less than a skill in interpersonal relations and communications. The only difference between following and leading is that, as a follower, you are more often on the receiving end of the communication, and as a leader you will initiate communication and action.

Leadership must be defined in terms of acceptance by others. You may have been given the title and the authority of a manager, but you are a leader only insofar as those under you accept your leadership. Most successful organizations recognize this and go to great lengths in selecting and training leaders for sensitive management positions. In fact, if an organization wants to grow, it *must* recognize and develop leaders.

To repeat: There are many naturally talented *potential* leaders, but no one is born with the experience necessary for leadership. If you are asking yourself whether or not you are a potential leader, and if you would enjoy the job, there is a simple answer. Review your Success Factors. If you have a talent for leadership, however latent, it will appear in many of your life and work achievements. It will almost always be more evident in how others react to you than in how you react to others.

Leadership is often related to control. True leadership will always mean that you are in control. However, being placed in a position of nominal control by an employer does not automatically make you a leader.

The first step in developing your leadership ability is to understand, both at the thinking and the feeling level, how people interact with each other. Observing your own reactions and those of others is excellent on-the-job training for this.

Much of the interaction between you as a leader and those under you takes place on the emotional level. Many employed men and women in the work world are said to have an "authority problem." While this may be true sometimes, most of the problem is caused by the inadequate training of managers in interpersonal relations.

Human reaction to events usually takes place on the emotional level first, as you know. This is, of course, true of the leader as well. If you are in a leadership position, it is your responsibility to deal not only with your emotional reactions, but also with those of your subordinates. Blowing off steam or blaming others are two natural and understandable reactions to an unfavorable situation, event, or statement. As a leader, you cannot afford the luxury of such reactions. Developing control of your feelings and reactions will put you in a position of control over those in your charge.

For example, you are required to see both sides of a dispute among your subordinates. If you become emotionally involved, you will lose control. You are not asked here to suppress your emotions but to channel them into positive, rational action. Develop this skill through daily practice.

If at any time you find yourself acting out a negative emotional reaction, you are declaring bankruptcy on your leadership and will have lost control. An extreme case might be threatening an employee with dismissal without careful, rational consideration. You may, on the other hand, make the decision to terminate the employment of such a person with good reason and after careful thought. In that case, the action is likely to benefit both the organization and the terminated employee, because he or she would be neither productive nor happy under the circumstances.

You must have a clear understanding and awareness of the mix of emotional reaction and rational judgment in all your decisions. This understanding is difficult to acquire, but the most successful leaders and managers have developed it to a high degree.

The constructive use of the emotions is, of course, an important tool in generating a spirit of cooperation and enthusiasm among your subordinates. Constant, genuine recognition of an employee as a person who is a contributing team member is one of the best management tools available to you.

All this may make it appear that the task of leadership is complex and difficult. It is! But the rewards gained from developing leadership skill and insight make this one of the most exciting of all career objectives for those who enjoy the varied challenges of human interaction.

Now let's look at the process of moving into a management position. As in every other form of career advancement, the steps with which you should by now be familiar are:

1. Getting information
2. Setting an objective
3. Communicating the objective
4. Implementing the objective and following through

If you have never been in a management position or other leadership role before, the first step is to find out what it means to carry leadership responsibility. Once again, your best sources of information are people who are successfully engaged in such an activity.

Assemble information that gives you a reasonably clear picture of the responsibilities and rewards of the leadership function, both by reading about it and by talking to a number of people who have found satisfaction and success in carrying out leadership responsibilities. Also review your Success Factors and career goals with regard to this information.

Here are questions you should be able to answer:

- Are you willing and able to take ultimate responsibility for a project or a group of people?
- While taking ultimate responsibility, are you able to delegate part of your work to others without losing control?
- Do you perceive the problems of those under you as a nuisance or as a challenging part of your job?
- Can you maintain a positive attitude toward others even under great pressure?
- Are you able to keep your emotions under control so that you can be a source of stability and reassurance to those under you?
- Have you been able to communicate your purposes to others in a way that motivates them to action?
- When you see a need or a job to be done in your area of responsibility, do you take the initiative or do you wait for others to act?
- When you see a job well done by others, are you in the habit of acknowledging it, and/or rewarding it? When is the last time you did so?
- Why do you want to be in a leadership position? Do you enjoy taking responsibility, solving problems, and working with and through others to achieve results? Or do you want to escape from working for others who have authority over you by becoming a "boss"? (It should be evident that a leadership role is not the answer to this last objective.)

Many of the answers to these questions will become clear when you review your past achievements (see Chapter 4). Even minor, early-life achievements will contain information on how you relate to other people, and how, when, and to what extent you enjoy taking responsibility and initiative. If you can find two achievements that answer each of the above questions in the affirmative, you have a basic leaning toward a leadership role and may wish to consider moving into such a role as the Next Step in your career.

If you have been in a leadership or management role, you will find it easy to corroborate your leadership ability or talent by reviewing your recent achievements. If there are none, you probably should reconsider your Next Step and evaluate all of your options. There are many rewarding positions in the world of work that do not involve leadership responsibility.

To set and implement a leadership or a management objective as part of a job search, follow the instructions given in the early chapters of this book.

Here are the guidelines for planning and carrying out a leadership/management objective as part of an internal campaign:

Once you have established clear lines of communications with your superiors and have decided on a career objective involving leadership responsibilities, you will be able to set specific goals. These goals must benefit both you and your employer. They must fill a need, provide a solution to a problem, or contribute to the accomplishment of a purpose both for you and the organization of which you are a part.

When you are in your new position of responsibility, you are once again ready to set objectives for the future. These objectives are the development of a leadership style, the establishment of relationships with your new subordinates as well as with your superiors, and the setting of work goals in line with your commitment to your employers.

Such objectives have value only if they are communicated, frequently, in both written and verbal form. Your subordinates, as well as your superiors, must be aware at all times of your purposes. They also need to be aware of how these purposes are being accomplished.

The following are important milestones in your progress

toward becoming an effective and respected leader and manager.

Start by establishing a climate of total, open communications with those under you. You have accomplished this when your subordinates feel comfortable in telling you the truth. This cannot be legislated; you will have to earn it. One of the best ways to earn it is to take the initiative and set an example in communicating openly and frequently with every person in your charge.

As soon as possible, become aware of the individual strengths and assets of your subordinates. Study their successes; encourage them to tell you about their accomplishments. In line with our well-tested and proven philosophy of concentrating on strengths before weaknesses, you will find it much easier to deal positively with the adverse factors of your employees once you know their strengths.

Train your subordinates in the human relations principles and techniques discussed in the two preceeding chapters. You needn't worry that you will encourage your employees to advance their careers outside your organization. On the contrary, thirty years of evidence proves that when these principles are correctly implemented, they increase your subordinates' security and loyalty to you.

One frequent concern of managers is that employees who are career-minded tend to ask for pay increases more frequently. This problem is easily avoided by applying the principle of performance before reward. Financial incentives by themselves are of very limited usefulness. Few managers resent providing compensation for demonstrated effectiveness. Always demand performance *before* discussing rewards, just as you would offer performance before asking for rewards for yourself. Apart from everything else, the reward will usually be greater if it is given for visible results, rather than for speculative anticipation.

Another important aspect of communications is their use in problem solving. Just as you wouldn't go to superiors with a problem without suggesting a solution, demand that subordinates come to you with solutions, rather than problems.

Every time someone brings a problem to you, ask him or her to make some kind of a suggestion for solving it. The suggested solution may not be the right one in every case, but the effort will instill in the other person a feeling of responsibility and participation in the decision-making process. This may require a lengthy educational process, but it will pay off. Your subordinates will gain a strong sense of their own worth from which they, you, and the entire organization will benefit.

Delegating responsibility to others is one of the most complex aspects of leadership. In many ways, the skill with which you do this is a real measure of your leadership ability. Delegating not only partial responsibility but actual decision-making power for a project, while you monitor progress and retain final control, requires judgement that must be developed gradually over a period of years. With an open system of communications and frequent feedback, not on demand but by habit, there is no danger in such delegation. Instead, it assures a strong, healthy organization. A manager who is afraid of having strong, capable, self-reliant people under him is not a leader.

This brings us to the concept of power. Managers who get satisfaction from using the authority vested in them without taking leadership responsibility are a millstone around the neck of any organization. One such manager can create a negative climate throughout an entire organization. This is first recognized by a slowdown of the growth rate of the organization and an increase in employee turnover. The management structure of many defunct business organizations has been poisoned by unskillful hiring and promotion of nonleaders.

It is essential that an organization take responsibility for training its leaders. It is possible to encourage successful leaders to set a climate where leadership skills are recognized and developed throughout the organization. This can be done through leadership seminars, workshops, and individual training.

Once again, it is important to recognize that day-to-day stability is just as much a responsibility of a leader as growth and development. How you deal with everyday problems is a mark of your leadership ability. Many major as well as minor problems create emotional waves. Remember, at the feeling level, there is very little difference between a major, minor, or mini problem. Very simply, the skilled leader will act to decrease the emotional wave, the unskilled leader and the non-leader will become emotionally involved in the problem and will reinforce the wave. In such a case, someone else will usually have to step in to bring things under control.

In the long run, there is no such thing as control by intimidation. Those who seek to establish control by such destructive means as threats, fear, and noncommunication are never successful for more than a day at a time. They will have to re-establish control anew every day, a back-breaking and unhappy task. Such people need career help. Increasingly, such help is available. But the aspiring manager who has a genuine instinct and liking for leadership and interpersonal relations can never be denied a leadership role.

15
Your Own Business

The greatest and most challenging test of your leadership ability may be the establishment and operation of your own business. At one time or another, most people have considered going into business for themselves. The rewards seem attractive: freedom, choice, control, being your own boss. But only about 4 percent of all those who try ever succeed in building and maintaining a profitable business.

This chapter will deal with the decision-making process leading to the establishment of your own business. The actual building of a business depends on the kind of business you are involved in, and it is beyond the scope of this book to provide detailed technical information on a variety of business ventures. But there are basic considerations and rules you must observe before you *start*. If you follow these guidelines, you will greatly increase your chances of being among the successful 4 percent.

The first of four points in considering a business venture of your own is: Why do you want to go into business for yourself? Ask yourself this question and answer it without reservations!

If the answer is that you have such a strong desire to *do* something that you can almost taste it, you are in excellent shape to get started. If, on the other hand, your motivation is derived mostly from a desire to *escape* from something, you are likely to run out of steam shortly after you have accomplished the actual escape. If you find yourself using phrases like "I'm tired of my job . . . of my boss . . . of working 9 to 5 . . . of working for others . . ." you are not ready to consider a business of your own.

Such negative motivators can be the starting point of the process, but they provide no strong *long-term* motivation for a business venture.

The second point you must consider is the range of your abilities. Your Success Factors, described in Chapter 4, are a reliable guide to your future ability to sustain an independent business venture. Factors like planning, organizing, independent decision making, judgment, and leadership verify the likelihood of your success. Success Factors that testify to your technical ability with regard to the business venture you are planning can be equally reliable. If necessary, associate with one or more people who have the Success Factors you may be lacking.

It should be clear that basic motivation and ability take precedence over purely mechanical factors, such as contacts, business knowledge, or capital. These can be acquired; basic motivation is almost impossible to procure. You either have it or you don't.

Emotional motivators, such as the desire to prove yourself or even the desire for financial independence, can be strong incentives. They may not always be reasonable, but they are real to you nevertheless. They must be combined with other factors mentioned above in order to lead to success.

The third point for consideration, and a basic requirement for any business venture, is your readiness to make sacrifices at the early stages to ensure success later.

You will not be working for a boss, but you will be working

for many people: your customers or clients. You will not be working 9 to 5, you will probably be working 8 A.M. to 10 P.M. or later. You won't be at the mercy of someone else's salary structure, you will be limited only by the income and expense structure of your business, which may mean that you may, at least at the beginning, be working for a salary that you wouldn't even consider if someone else offered it to you. You will have lots of authority, accompanied by lots of responsibility. But you *will* be making your own decisions. And if you do everything right, you will reap vast benefits.

There is a fourth point to consider: Are you a developer or a maintainer? Of course, most of us are developers and maintainers at the same time. But we all have at least a slight preference in one direction or the other.

A successful business needs both: developers to start, build, and expand it; maintainers to give it strength and structure. Your Success Factors are a reliable guide to your own preferences. Once you have recognized your success pattern, it becomes simply a matter of acquiring a partner or a key employee who supplies the Success Factors that most effectively complement your own.

So-called entrepreneurs are frequently very successful in creating a new business, but they just as frequently cause the business to disintegrate after a period of time. An entrepreneur is an extreme form of builder or developer and seldom has talent or flair for maintaining a structure. Because few entrepreneurs recognize this, they are unwilling to delegate the operational maintenance functions to others and, therefore, become heavy contributors to the failure statistics.

Let's take a look at the two steps needed to build the foundation for a successful business venture of your own.

Step number one, as always, is to set an objective. You can always revise it later, but you must focus on a purpose and that purpose must be a positive one. Review your Success Factors as well as your experience. Don't ignore your feelings. Unless your emotions are in line with your purpose, you will not be successful. Make sure you have considered the four points listed above.

The second step is to make contacts, and simultaneously do the research necessary to give you a clear picture of the opportunities as well as the problems you are likely to face. At the same time you will "reality-test" your prior knowledge and your assumptions in relation to your objective.

There is only one reliable source for realistic, up-to-date information: people who are currently successful *and* happy in the kind of business you are planning to build for yourself. Success in a business venture is not always synonymous with personal success in this area of the work world. Some people lose control of their own business, while the business itself is continuing to do well. Such people are unreliable sources of information.

In the process of doing this personalized research, you will also build an important contact network (as outlined in Chapter 6).

One word of caution: Consider the source of any negative advice and information carefully. The person providing this information may see you as a future competitor. Our experience has shown that successful and secure business owners are seldom deterred by fear of competition from being helpful to others. In fact, given half a chance, most people will go to inspiring lengths to be helpful. If you have experiences to the contrary, review your own approaches and attitudes toward others.

The following are major subjects on which you will be seeking information. There is no particular order to this research, and the information sources include both word of mouth and published materials.

- Contact individuals who operate successful businesses in your chosen field and ask them about the reasons for their success. Find out about possible pitfalls in building such a business. Concentrate on getting advice and information about how to recognize and solve problems effectively or prevent them altogether. Ask to see financial statements (although you may not always get them).

- Capital investment is an important subject in planning a business venture, and accurate information in this area can be crucial. Undercapitalization is a frequent reason for business failure. However, in most of those cases, it only happens to be the most conspicuous aspect of the failure. Other factors remain unrecognized, which accounts for the fact that a number of people fail again and again in the same business area, regardless of how much money they have at their disposal.

- If you have been told that you should abandon any idea of going into business for yourself unless you are independently wealthy, ignore the advice. In most cases, you should not use your own money, even if you have large quantities of it. Your success in getting financing for your venture is also a good way to reality-test your objective. Given the number of people in this country who want to invest money, if you can't convince someone else to invest in your venture, your plan may not be sound.

A reasonable approach would be to consider a limited investment, if your research tells you it would make sense. But don't, by any means, abandon your plans because of lack of funding. A search for capital can easily be built into your Referral campaign. People with money to invest are far more plentiful than people with talent.

Different types of businesses require different types and

amounts of investment. This ranges from a manufacturing business, with its need for fixed premises and equipment, at one end of the scale, to a consulting or service business, with very little need for either, at the other end.

• There is another type of investment that has to be considered: time and energy. This investment frequently also has a financial side, because the remuneration may be small by comparison. Given a sound plan, the rewards later on can be great. But you must enter a business venture with your eyes open. Find out, from others who have had personal experience, what is required in terms of time and energy.

• Another type of investment needed is your basic knowledge of the tools of the trade. Because this is one of the most important factors of business success, some guidelines are needed:

A liking for good food is not enough reason to open a restaurant. Nor is an ability to cook. You can always hire a good cook. The restaurant business is complex and highly competitive. The failure rate is high. Unless you have had firsthand experience, it is difficult to gain the knowledge necessary to build a successful food service business. You can't get it secondhand. You can obtain experience in any business by becoming an employee in that business and studying its inner workings. As a matter of fact, your constructive attitude, based on your personal commitment, will make you a very valuable employee. And your chances for advancing rapidly, and getting a close look at the firm's management structure, are excellent.

The length of time or amount of exposure needed varies with the type of business and your ability to absorb information.

While you gather the necessary information, start building

a relationship with legal and financial advisors. You will always do better if you have professional help available to you when you need it. If you wait until you need it, it's too late to start looking for the right people. Every person running a business profits from knowing what legal options and problems he or she may have. In addition, the benefits of good financial and tax advice are obvious and begin even before you start your venture.

Use a word-of-mouth approach to find a lawyer and an accountant who are successfully experienced in your field of business. Also, develop a relationship with the manager of a bank, who can help you finance your business when capital is needed.

Make sure you can communicate easily with the people you expect to deal with. The investment in building such relationships is minimal compared to the later benefits, both in finances and peace of mind.

If you are currently employed, you can do most of the things described above while you are still working in your job. Unless you have an independent income, it is rarely a good idea to begin the business from a standstill. Even the actual start of the business can happen on a gradual basis.

If your business area is one of service or consulting, it is frequently possible to take on a few clients on the side, and then take the step from your current job to your new business when you have built up enough income to provide adequate support. Many tax accountants start their independent business ventures in this way.

When you are ready to start your new business venture, one of your first challenges will be staffing. Even a small service business frequently requires secretarial help, almost from the beginning. While it is often a good idea to go into business *for* yourself, it rarely is advisable to be in business *by* yourself. Partners and key employees play an important part in the success of a business organization. They need to be able to work as a team.

A prevalent temptation for any business owner is to hire people like himself. Thereby, he multiplies his strengths as well as his weaknesses. Make a practice of hiring people who complement you in the areas where you need help.

Always consider taking on a partner. Few people, especially in a highly specialized business area, have both the technical know-how and the management talent to keep such a business afloat. The owner and president of a well-known New England-based optical company demonstrated this when he surrounded himself with highly qualified optical engineers, duplicating and multiplying his own field of expertise. The firm fell victim to a multitude of human relations problems. No one knew how to deal with them, and the company is no longer in business.

The information on career follow-through given in preceding chapters applies heavily to you if you own and manage a business. Once the survival and growth of your business dictates your priorities, you are in danger of losing control over your career. Many people who became our clients had found that they had delegated all desirable functions in their organizations to others. They were cemented into jobs they wouldn't have accepted at any price if someone else had owned the company.

All of that having been said, business ownership, in the long run, is all its most ardent champions say it is. But only if all the advice given in this chapter is followed, and only if you are ready to make the commitment and sacrifices required to build a sound, growing, and profitable organization.

16
Questions and Answers

Here are brief answers to the questions most often asked by job and career seekers. All of these answers are discussed in more detail throughout this book.

Q: How do I know what kind of job I should be looking for?
A: The only right job for you is one that allows you to use the skills and talents you have enjoyed using all your life.

Q: How do I know what my greatest abilities, skills, and talents are?
A: By writing down ten to fifteen achievements, things you did that gave you enjoyment and satisfaction, whether or not they were acknowledged by others. You will recognize a pattern of abilities that is common to many of your achievements.

Q: How do I find out which jobs need the skills I have?
A: Once you have decided which of your skills or Success Factors are the ones you most want to use, make a list of jobs that appear to use them. Every time you read a newspaper or a magazine, watch television or talk to people, you will find your personal radar working. Public and business libraries are also excellent sources of information. Gradually you will get more and more detailed information about the career field that most closely matches your interests and abilities.

Q: How do I find out about job openings?

A: In addition to the job openings that are advertised, all jobs that are currently filled are *potentially* available due to normal turnover. (The average length of time a job is held by one person is four to four and a half years.) The more people who are doing the kind of work you are looking for, the more chance you have of getting one of those jobs.

Q: How do I go about getting the job?

A: By meeting, talking with, and being known by the people who can give you a job. The *only* way to find a job is *through people!*

Q: How do I get to the people who can give me a job?

A: There are a number of ways to meet such people, and you should use them in combinations. The easiest and most effective way is to be referred or introduced to them by people you already know. Another is by answering ads, or working with an employment agency; the least effective way is to write confetti letters or knock on doors.

Q: I'm not aggressive; I have difficulty meeting people. How can I overcome this problem?

A: There is no need to be aggressive. Sometimes it can hurt you. What you need is a purpose in everything you do. A clear purpose, or objective, whether you are going into an interview or a job, will give you all the confidence you need.

Q: Isn't it easier to find a job through answering an ad or going to an employment agency?

A: If your job objective is a profession in which many jobs are advertised, use these approaches. But all recent studies show that the vast majority of the better jobs are obtained by people through word of mouth and are *never* published anywhere or listed with employment agencies.

QUESTIONS AND ANSWERS   223

Q: Why are my chances of getting a job through word of mouth better than getting one through an ad or agency?

A: When you are being considered for a job you heard about by word of mouth, you are usually one of very few candidates, and sometimes the only one, to be considered. Once a job has been published in a newspaper or listed with agencies, you may be competing with twenty or thirty other people, and sometimes with hundreds. Also, the best jobs do not remain vacant long enough to be published.

Q: Are "contacts" people who can give me a job?

A: No. The best way to meet people who can hire you is by introduction or referral from someone else. So almost any person you know can be a starting "contact." You can then get from your starting or primary contacts to the people who are in a position to offer you a job. This is known as the *Referral* method.

Q: Is it risky and expensive to change careers?

A: In most cases, no. You will be moving from a job or career that does not make full use of your best skills and talents to one that does. By definition, you will be more productive, and therefore more valuable in your new career. You will also learn faster because you will be more motivated. Lack of work experience won't hold you back long.

Q: What is a career?

A: Ideally, a career is an increasingly satisfying and rewarding series of jobs or assignments that allow you to use your greatest strengths, abilities, skills, and talents, known as Success Factors.

Q: Why is it necessary to plan a career?

A: In order to make sure that you will have rewarding work to do every day of your life, you must be able to make intelligent job choices. By leaving your career to accidents, you are turning control over to other people who have no knowledge of or interest in your career goals.

Q: In planning a career, should I take into consideration only career fields that provide the most opportunities, jobs, money, and recognition?

A: Do not let fluctuating job market and economic factors control your career choice.

There are *two* steps in career planning. The first one is *What* will you do? And the second, *Where* will you do it? First decide what functions should be part of your work, what skills and abilities you will be using and developing. Only after this step is completed should you consider alternative job environments.

Q: As a woman, should I plan my career in a field usually associated with women, or should I try to break into other fields?

A: Same as the last answer. Your career choices and decisions must be dictated by your Success Factors.

Q: If I'm happy in my work, why should I worry about career goals?

A: You need career checkups just as you need medical checkups, at least once a year. Review your progress to see if you are on track and revise your career objective in light of new insights you might have gained. You may need to take on new challenges periodically to keep enjoying your work.

Q: If my career isn't showing any progress, and I am still at the same point I was a year ago, should I change jobs?

A: Not necessarily. Most employers will give you an opportunity to advance your career on the job, if you take the initiative.

Q: Is it a good idea to turn my hobby into a vocation?

A: Sometimes what makes a vocation enjoyable is the lack of structure and financial pressure. Rather than translating your hobby directly into an income-producing business activity, identify the Success Factors you use in your avocation, and make them the basis for your Next Step.

Q: Will lack of experience disqualify me from the job I want?

A: Not unless both you and the person who interviews you believe it does. There are many factors that make you able to do a job; experience is only one of them.

Q: How can a student get enough information about job requirements to plan a career?

A: Everyone is willing to give advice and information to young people. The problem is that most of this advice is useless, because it is unstructured and rarely hits the mark. Take charge of gathering the information you need by asking the people who are most likely to have it, the people who have found success and satisfaction in their career field. You will rarely be refused.

Q: Does it make sense for a student to engage in career planning?

A: Absolutely. Even though you shouldn't think in terms of planning the entire course of your career (or your life), become aware of your Success Factors so you can be sure to start out in the right direction. Many career problems and years of needless suffering are caused by getting locked into a wrong career virtually by accident.

Q: Is it easy nowadays to change careers?

A: It is never easy, but the rewards are sizable. It can take from several weeks to a year to complete a career change. But it is a small price to pay in light of the many years of being happy and productive, doing work you enjoy and earning more recognition than ever before.

Q: Can employment agencies help me or advise me in changing my career?

A: Not usually. In most cases, employment agencies are paid by the employer. The employer takes a risk, however small, in employing a person who is embarking on a new career. An agency cannot ethically be expected to take that risk for the employer.

Q: How will not having a college degree affect my career plans?
A: You base your career plans on what you have, not what you don't have. There will be many ways to convince an employer that you can do a job. For every lack, substitute a strength. But if a degree is a legal requirement, as in medicine, consider getting one.

Q: What if a career is closed to me for any reason?
A: There are alternative positions in most career fields, where the requirements are less strict, such as paramedical and paralegal positions. If poor eyesight prevents you from becoming a jet pilot, there are many jobs related to airplanes or to flying that do not require perfect eyesight.

Q: I am bored with my job. Should I change careers?
A: You should certainly review your job in relation to your career goals. Having done that, you have three remedies available to you: an Internal campaign, a job change, or a career change.

Q: Can I get help in planning a career or making a career change?
A: Two kinds of help are available: books and career counselors.

   The quality of the books on career subjects is on the increase, but make sure the person who wrote the book you use has at least ten years of career counseling experience. Career counseling is a highly skilled profession, and much damage is being done by amateurs.

   Books can supply the basic tools. They cannot generate or sustain your motivation, or deal with special day-to-day problems during the implementation phase of your career plan. Only an experienced, professional career counselor can do this.

Q: What information should be given in a resume?
A: A job objective that communicates your purpose to the reader,

and proof that you can carry out that purpose. Everything else is superfluous.

Q: Is it wise to stick to a standard format in writing your resume?
A: Only if you think of yourself as a standard person and want a standard job. Most employers at the decision-making level are looking for unique individuals and are bored with standard resumes.

Q: Does everybody need a resume?
A: Yes! What's more, everyone needs to *write* a resume. Everyone needs a purpose. A well-written resume is one of the best ways to communicate your purpose in writing. Only when you have gone through the process of putting your job and career objectives and supporting statements on paper, can you be sure that you are prepared to communicate your value to a future employer.

Q: Which is more important in a resume, content or appearance?
A: Both!

Q: What happens if some of the dates on my resume turn an interviewer off?
A: Leave out anything that can be interpreted negatively. Give only positive information. You can give the other information during the interview, where you can deal with any negative reactions in person.

Q: How can I tell if my resume is good?
A: If it helps you get interviews, it's good. Also, you will be told. People might not tell you they don't like your resume, but they *will* tell you if they like it. If you get no positive comments, tear it up and start over.

Q: Isn't it better to leave off the job objective? Wouldn't I then be considered for a wider range of opportunities?
A: You would also run the risk of being thought to have no pur-

pose in your work and to be a jack-of-all-trades. You are safe if you describe the skills you want to use and stay away from titles and tight job descriptions.

Q: Should I consider a different resume for every interviewer?

A: No. Before you go on the interview, you won't have enough information no matter how much research you do. After you have established contact, you no longer need a resume for that person. Both your face-to-face interviews and your thank-you letters are much better means to adapt yourself to the needs of the organization, so far as is compatible with your career objective.

Q: Is it really necessary to write thank-you letters to everyone?

A: It is the best value-for-effort-invested you have in the *entire* job and career building process. Thank-you letters have powerful, lasting impact and are written much too infrequently by most people.

Q: Is it better to say thank you in person or in a letter?

A: Both. A letter will get your thoughts across clearly. Personal follow-up can add the force of positive emotions. Any time you want to communicate an idea, the combination of writing and talking is the most effective method.

Q: I've answered many blind job ads—in most cases, I never get a response. Why?

A: With hundreds of people answering just a single ad, it is not reasonable to expect the sponsoring organization to respond to more than a few applicants. The advertiser is using the volume approach. You can do the same. Answer all ads remotely related to your job objective. The investment should be small, and the return can be maximized by sending out very brief, well-focused letters.

Q: What if the job market is tight in my field?

A: First, don't take anyone's word for that until you have talked to a number of successful people in your field. Then if there is indeed a dearth of jobs or low turnover, decide how much time and effort you can afford to spend on a concentrated market campaign. Consider shifting your target to a related field where you can still make the best possible use of your Success Factors.

Q: Is the Christmas season a poor time to look for a job?

A: No. Many hiring decisions are made during December. The first of the year is a popular time to start employment. Also, in many organizations, activity slows down before the holiday season, and many people are in a better frame of mind to give interviews.

Q: How much do unemployment figures affect my chances of finding a job?

A: Less than is generally assumed. The impact of such statistics is largely emotional. People are affected more by their reaction to the facts than by the facts themselves.

Most unemployment statistics are general. You will usually find that a tiny percentage of any given figure actually applies to your population category and career field. To counteract the emotional reaction, which can have a very negative impact on your attitude, visualize 7 percent unemployment as 93 percent employment.

Q: How do I know if I would be successful in a business of my own?

A: The best information on the requirements, problems, and opportunities of a business comes from people who have been successful themselves. Your past achievements and Success Factors are a reliable guide to your ability to carry the responsibility involved.

Q: What is the best way to deal with employment application forms?

A: Give only positive information, or state the information you give in positive terms. Relate experience in terms of specific accomplishments, and emphasize your Success Factors. Avoid giving information that can be interpreted negatively; instead substitute: "To be discussed during interview," or a similar phrase (blank spaces tend to irritate users of such forms). In order to retain control, never give confidential information, such as income history or salary expectations, except where it is required in civil service applications.

Whenever possible, rather than dealing with application forms, use the Referral method outlined in this book to identify and meet a person for whom you want to work. Once you have accomplished this, filling out a form will become a mere formality and will not get in the way of the hiring process. This is even true of civil service applications.

Q: Is filling out forms the only way to get a government job?
A: Government, as well as all other sectors of the work world, is made up of people and governed by the same principles of human relations. Taking the initiative, researching options, and, as always, making contact with people is the road to success. The quality of your contact network, more than your skill in filling out forms, produces results.

Q: Is the formal approach to an academic appointment the only route?
A: See just above.

Q: Why should anyone give me an interview if he doesn't have a job opening for me?
A: Everyone in a position to make hiring decisions always faces the problem of losing good people and having to replace them. When an employee gives notice, it is, in many cases, too late to start looking for a replacement. Most key people in organizations welcome the opportunity to meet someone who could solve such a future problem for them. Make it absolutely clear

that you don't expect a job offer at this time. If you have been referred by a person your interviewer knows, he or she will be doubly motivated to see you.

Q: What is assertiveness?

A: Assertiveness is having a positive purpose in everything you say and do, believing in that purpose, and being able to communicate it to others. It is not aggressiveness, which has a hostile component.

Q: Do interviewers have a right to ask me personal questions?

A: Right or not, such questions are sometimes asked. You can best protect your privacy and assert yourself by the answers you give, not by judging whether or not the question is permissible.

Q: During interviews I'm worried about being asked about experience and education I don't have. How should I answer those questions?

A: Interviewers don't ask such questions to trap you or annoy you. They want to find out if there is any question about your being able to do the job. Always give positive answers. For instance, if you are asked about work experience you don't have, give an example of related experience, or show that you have been successful using some of the same abilities that this job requires. If you have done your homework, you can substitute a strength for every seeming weakness.

Q: How should I dress for interviews?

A: Conservatively, and with care. It is perceived as a compliment to the interviewer if you have taken some trouble in choosing the clothes you wear on interviews. And it makes you feel more confident. When in doubt, dress like the successful people in your field.

Q: Does the first impression I make on the interviewer decide the quality of the whole interview?

A: Not necessarily. Of course you will do everything you can to make a favorable first impression, such as arriving early for the interview. But you will have many opportunities to establish rapport, and it is the overall impression you make that counts.

Q: Is it ethical to look for a job while I am working?
A: Yes. It is only unethical to stop doing useful work for your employer while accepting payment. It is also a good idea to give your employer an opportunity to improve your working conditions, if it's in his power to do so, before you look for another job, or before you accept one.

Q: If I miss out on a job opportunity and someone else is hired, should I give up on that employer?
A: By no means. The fact that you were considered shows that the employer was interested in you. This may mean that you have your foot in the door for the next opportunity, especially if you came close. Take the initiative. Show the employer you do not feel rejected.

Q: How much time should an interview take?
A: About twenty to forty-five minutes, unless the interviewer decides to extend it beyond that.

Q: I have a serious health problem. Should I tell my interviewer about it?
A: Not until you have been made an offer. If you bring it up at the beginning, you will make it difficult for an interviewer to focus on the really important things, such as whether or not you can do the job. After the interviewer has decided you are right for the position, and makes you an offer, there is usually no danger in bringing up the problem. In fact, it will be appreciated. It would be considered unfair to accept a job without telling your future employer about a former alcohol problem, serious mental problem, or prison record.

Q: Why do interviewers ask so many questions about my relationships with former bosses, associates, and subordinates?

A: Every employer knows that qualifications for a job must include your ability to work well with the people in his or her organization, otherwise the other qualifications are of very little use.

Q: I'm often told that I am overqualified for a job. Is this a polite way of being turned down?

A: In most cases, no. It is a legitimate cause for concern, though. An interviewer who uses this phrase usually feels you may lose interest in the job soon and will leave after a short period of employment. By stating a possible problem, the interviewer is usually inviting you to persuade him that it is not a problem.

Q: How can I tell during an interview if I'm being seriously considered for a job?

A: There are a number of green lights, such as an unusually long and positive interview, being shown around the premises, being questioned closely in a specific area of your experience, and being invited to return for a second interview.

Q: If I'm being offered a job, but compensation is not mentioned, should I bring up the subject?

A: No. Money will be mentioned sooner or later. The more time you have to convince your interviewer of your ability and positive attitude, the better your bargaining position will be when the subject of remuneration does come up.

Q: Isn't it better not to appear too anxious or too enthusiastic about a job opportunity?

A: Although many "cocktail career counselors" advocate this, it is a myth. The more enthusiasm you display, the more certain your interviewer will be of your long-range motivation and ability to perform. Enthusiasm actually makes you a more valu-

able candidate. It also puts you in a stronger negotiating position. You will be able to drive a hard bargain, because you will
look very much better than most other candidates for the job,
who probably labor under the above misconception.

Q: How do I know what I'm worth?
A: You are worth the highest dollar amount any employer is willing and able to pay you.

Q: Isn't it good to have at least a general idea what the average
person in similar positions is being paid?
A: There is little harm in researching this, as long as your purpose
is to guard against accepting a blatantly low offer. If you are
using your Success Factors, you are neither an average person
nor will you just do an average job. Having read this book, you
are also much better prepared for negotiating a good salary
than the average job seeker.

Q: Are all salary offers negotiable?
A: Not all, but more are than is generally realized. When in doubt,
assume that the salary figure offered is open for further discussion.

Q: If the highest salary offer for a job is not acceptable to me, is
there any point in continuing the discussion?
A: Yes. It takes only a minute to turn down a job, and there is always time to do that. There are many ways in which an employer can sweeten the pot, including some form of profit sharing or substantial future salary increases. It is up to you to
explore the possibilities.

Q: Should I tell interviewers what my current or past salary was
when I'm asked?
A: No. It will eliminate most of your chances of negotiating a high-
er-than-average starting salary in the new job. The same applies if you are asked to state your salary requirements.

Q: Won't I run the risk of antagonizing an interviewer by not revealing my income history?

A: Not if it is done with courtesy and if you state your willingness to fit into the future employer's income structure.

Q: If I travel to another city for an interview, who pays my expenses?

A: The person or organization who issues the invitation expects to pay your expenses, unless stated otherwise. If you have asked for the interview, and there is no specific job opening available, you will usually have to pay your own expenses. When in doubt, clarify the issue before you go.

Q: If I have a business lunch or dinner with another person, who pays the check?

A: The person who issued the invitation.

Q: Is it difficult to relocate to another part of the country and get a job there?

A: Not as difficult as most people believe, provided the move is planned carefully. In most cases, there is no need to wait until you have completed your move to start a market campaign.

Q: Are office politics a necessary part of my working life?

A: Positive, constructive politics—such as solving problems, helping people advance, building positive attitudes and communications—is an essential part of job and career advancement. Negative or destructive politics—such as diminishing others, cutting off communications, creating problems, and reinforcing negative trends and attitudes—sometimes appears to produce action in the short run, but never succeeds in the long run. If you have any doubts, study people who are successful and happy in their work.

Q: What can I do about an incompetent and dishonest boss?

A: First, realize that you are probably the victim of an emotional oversimplification. Then try to get a balanced picture of all your boss's strengths and weaknesses. Write them down. Following that, take the initiative to rebuild positive communications with your boss by acknowledging one or more of his or her strengths.

There is always time to implement an Internal campaign or a market campaign later, but first try the above. If you succeed in rebuilding your relationship with your boss, it means you are really in control of your environment, and sooner or later you will need to develop your ability to gain such control.

Q: If I seriously disagree with my boss, or feel I have been unfairly treated, should I always tell him so?

A: Always! But choose your method and timing very carefully. Don't give in to emotional impulses to blow off steam. Getting things out of your system isn't nearly as beneficial as achieving a positive resolution to a problem.

Q: Do feelings always get in the way of rational behavior on the job?

A: No. Positive feelings are essential to the achievement of anything worthwhile. They are the fuel that powers positive thought and positive action.

Q: Does more money always mean more pressure in a job?

A: More money frequently means more responsibility. This includes the responsibility to organize your job so that pressure doesn't build up, and you remain in control.

Q: I've done a good job, but I'm not getting the recognition I deserve. What should I do?

A: It is not enough to do a good job: you must also be seen to be doing a good job. Your superiors must be aware of your contributions. It is your responsibility to see that they are informed by communicating with them frequently.

Also, make sure that you and your boss agree on what you call a good job. Hard work by itself is no virtue unless your purposes and those of your employer are identical.

Q: Is it difficult for a woman who has worked in the home for many years to enter or re-enter the job market?

A: It requires a great deal of preparation. Generate job offers by demonstrating how the abilities and talents you used in the home can be applied to a new career. Many jobs in the world of work require an ability to organize, coordinate, and make decisions, as well as a talent for creative thinking, dealing with people, and communicating. These are among the skills usually developed to a high degree by homemakers.

Q: How difficult is it to change from a military career to a civilian one?

A: See just above.

Q: How realistic is it to have two concurrent jobs in order to make ends meet?

A: Most people who end up in such a situation have two jobs and no career. Building a career takes total, undivided commitment to making each successive job advance toward an ideal goal. Few people have been able to build any kind of satisfaction or noticeable career advancement while holding concurrent jobs.

There are, of course, other ways to do two jobs without interfering with career development—for example, when such jobs complement each other and can be described as "two-pronged career advancement." There is also a job and a supporting program of study, or a job combined with responsibilities in the home.

Q: How do I handle age discrimination in the job market?

A: By stressing the positive aspects of your age. If you are past middle age, you can offer many years of valuable experience and tested judgment. If you are just starting out in a career, you can offer youth, flexibility, energy, and the ability to learn.

Problems of this kind are made worse by many job seekers'

own adverse attitudes and prejudices. They often communicate negative factors without balancing the picture with positive factors. Age, youth, no degree, or a Ph.D. in themselves are not assets but can become assets in the right context. Even the lack of a degree can be described in terms of emphasis on practical, on-the-job experience. Another attitudinal problem is the firm belief of many job seekers that discrimination is a fact of life and that nothing can be done to remedy it. Such people are defeated before they start.

Q: How can I avoid prejudice in the job market?
A: By developing the skill to generate prejudice *in your favor*. Once someone has a bias in favor of your strengths, automatic prejudice against factors you are not able to control will eliminate itself.

Q: How can I cope better with having been fired.
A: Start by dealing with your feelings. Recognize that feelings of hostility toward others burn up valuable energy and produce nothing. Your seeming loss of self-worth is a real feeling, but it is not a "real" fact.

Then swing into full-time productive planning and action. Enlist the help of your family and friends. Instead of being an object of pity, you will become an inspiration to them. With good planning, the results you get will be directly proportional to your positive attitude.

Q: Do I need to be concerned about my "image"?
A: With or without your concern, you will make an impression on others. You can constructively influence the picture others have of you without being accused of vanity.

By consciously acting in a positive and responsible manner, by developing a reputation for positive self-control, for punctuality, courtesy, and for fairness to others you can propel your career ahead immeasurably. You might start tomorrow morning by arriving at your job with a smile.

Index

239